THE DEMOCRATIC PROCESS IN A
DEVELOPING SOCIETY

THE DEMOCRATIC PROCESS IN A DEVELOPING SOCIETY

A. H. Somjee

© A. H. Somjee 1979

First published 1979 by
THE MACMILLAN PRESS LTD
London and Basingstoke
Associated companies in Delhi
Dublin Hong Kong Johannesburg Lagos
Melbourne New York Singapore Tokyo

Printed in Great Britain by
REDWOOD BURN LTD,
Trowbridge and Esher

British Library Cataloguing in Publication Data

Somjee, Abdulkarim Husseinbhoy
   The democratic process in a developing society
   1. Political participation – India
   2. Underdeveloped areas – Political participation
   – Case studies
   I. Title
   301.5'92   JQ281

   ISBN 0-333-26778-8

Contents

Preface

This book is about the constraints and problems which developing societies face, or will face, when they attempt to make the exercise of political power representative and accountable. Although so far very few of these societies have been able to sustain and strengthen their liberal institutions, their gradual democratisation is as likely to take place as their economic modernisation. In that respect the democratic experience of India – with all the constraints of social hierarchy, economic poverty and traditional attitude to authority, on the one hand, and the attempts to make political participation an instrument for solving the basic problems of society, on the other – becomes quite significant. For in their attempts to make their governments more accountable they, too, will face constraints and problems more or less similar to those of India, though their approach to these problems will no doubt be different.

In the industrialised countries of the West, economic development, urbanisation and some measure of social equality preceded the formation of democratic institutions. In some of the developing countries, on the other hand, this process has been reversed. There, the strategy of economic development at the expense of political liberalisation has not found many supporters. For such countries a slow pace of economic advancement, through the democratic process, is not the only problem. Ethnic and class constraints, permitting only an inhibited form of political participation, present a real problem. This study will examine the gradual process whereby the people of a developing society overcome some of the obstacles to their participation and develop the capacity to gradually use it to tackle the problems of hierarchy, poverty and fear of government.

In order to examine this phenomenon as realistically as possible, I have concentrated on a single community. For over a decade, from

1966 to 1977, I interviewed the *same* individuals, so that I could see for myself how their capacity to participate in the democratic process grew, and how they began to use it to solve some of their problems. In a sense I have concentrated on the human aspect of their political development.

The term democratic process, as referred to in this study, calls for an explanation. Robert Dahl has suggested that it is essentially concerned with two sets of related activities: exercising influence on leaders; and making governments responsive and accountable. Within the situation of a developing country like India, however, the term democratic process has to mean more than that. To be able to attain the position referred to by Dahl, first of all the individual must be released from the constraints of the primary groups to which he is born so that he may exercise his political choice in an uninhibited fashion. Simultaneously, the democratic process has to help him to grow in understanding and capacity, so that, by trial and error and working in concert with his fellow men, he can learn to use his new political status to demand effective solutions to the problems which afflict them.

In preparing this study, which is based on extended field-work, I have been assisted by more people than I can possibly acknowledge here. In particular I want to thank the team of research assistants who each year helped me to collect data on the growing maturity of the people in our random sample. They were Geeta Patel, Ila and Vimla Maharawal, Daksha Kapadia, Arun Brahmabhatta, Rashmi Trivedi, Rajnikant Patel, Ramanbhai Prajapati, Harish Bhatt, Kaushik and Ramesh Parikh. Thanks are also due to Madhukar Maharaja for his help in preparing the stratified sample, to Marjori Polvi for computer analysis, and to Elsie Trott, K. G. B. Nair, Violet Goodwill and Marie Dombowsky for typing the manuscript. I am particularly grateful to the Warden of Queen Elizabeth House, Oxford, for affiliation during my research leave and to Lady (Ursula) Hicks for making her study available to me when I was working on the final draft of this book.

This, the fruit of several years' work, could have been neither undertaken nor completed without the travel and research grants provided by the Canada Council. Thanks are also due to the President's Research Grant at Simon Fraser University, and to the Shastri Indo-Canadian Institute for the occasional research grants they also made.

In preparing the manuscript I benefited a great deal from my discussions with Norman Palmer, the doyen of American scholars in Indian studies; and my wife, Geeta Somjee, was closely associated with this work, too, and, but for her constant encouragement and help, I could not have completed it.

West Vancouver   A. H. Somjee
1979

1 Traditional Society through the Crucible of the Democratic Process

For the first time in its history, Western democratic theory has been confronted by a non-Western democratic experience which has not only questioned some of its underlying assumptions, but has also cast doubts on the efficacy of some of its conceptual tools. Such a challenge has come from the Indian democratic experiment of the second half of this century. Like most other social and political theories, theories about democracy are deeply grounded in the political history and tradition of the countries of the West, and, with the exception of a few scholars working in the field of comparative government or political development, such a challenge to their universal validity has largely gone unnoticed.

The reasons for such an insensitivity are not far to seek. For one thing, attempts to theorise about democratic experiences, even those of the Western countries, often get bogged down in interminable controversies, leaving scholars in the field little time to face fresh challenges to their theoretical formulations. Then there is the question of how substantial the gains of the non-Western world have been in making the exercise of political power representational and accountable there. But more than anything else the insensitivity of democratic theorists seems to stem from the assumption that unless the conditions which gave rise to democratic institutions in eighteenth- and nineteenth-century Europe and America, can be replicated in the non-Western world, any attempt to transplant or superimpose such institutions there will not get off the ground.

The non-Western world itself is engaged in 'century-skipping', and the desire to democratise political power on the part of its elite is as strong as its desire to raise the standard of living or introduce an increasing measure of equality. Despite setbacks and reversals the non-Western world may not necessarily follow the 'Euro-American route', nor require an equivalent time-span to politically modernise itself.

In this respect the experience of India is most significant. Her democratic development was *not* a function of her economic modernisation. On the contrary, in India's case the growth of political participation became a powerful force in demanding (though not always effectively) a faster rate of economic development and simultaneously, a more responsible use of political power. The attempt on the part of her rulers to over-emphasise the one at the expense of the other in the 1960s and 1970s, did not go down well with a people experiencing greater political participation and a deeper realisation of the essentially instrumental character of state power. A vastly enhanced and demanding political participation successfully reaffirmed its demand for both through the general election of 1977.

All over the non-Western world, and particularly in the Indian sub-continent, there has been a revival of movements towards political participation after a spell of illiberalism which promised much and achieved very little. The performance of the repressive regimes there has convinced the electorate that there are no short-cuts to all-round development and that first of all those who exercise political power must be made responsible to the people and their system of laws.

Within the non-Western world itself, India has emerged as a country where political participation has not only been able to check the arbitrary exercise of power, but is also beginning to generate effective pressure towards economic development and some measure of distributive justice. In its emergence as a vital instrument of social change, political participation has had to overcome a number of constraints put upon it by the primary groups that one finds in traditional societies. This book is a study of its growing ability to overcome those constraints and become a secular force in her society and politics.

Ever since Baron de Montesquieu published his classic *The Spirit of Laws* describing political institutions as an epiphenomenon of the delicate balance of seven forces – climate, religion, laws, maxims of government, precedents, morals and customs – social scientists have often wondered whether the new nations, at crucial moments in their history, were free to *choose* their own political institutions and begin their political destiny anew. Montesquieu himself ruled out such a possibility. For him climate and historical tradition, over which one can have no control and therefore from which there is no escape, stood in causal relationship with the political institutions that a country finally comes to have.

A century after him, in *Democracy in America* (1889), Alex de Tocqueville evaluated the philosophical assumptions and performance of the deliberately chosen new political institutions of the USA, and was deeply apprehensive for the future survival of the democratic republic and the union. In the long run, in his view, democracy in the USA might be found wanting, and might even become unworkable in practice.

When de Tocqueville was engaged in evaluating the suitability of democracy to the USA, the country, after nearly 100 years of existence, was not over the hump of its internal storms and stresses. He deeply admired the vigour of the young American nation and its abiding faith in the ideology of democracy but wondered how far internal problems would allow such a form of government to persist. In de Tocqueville's view, 'Democracy appears to be much better adapted for the peaceful conduct of society, or for an *occasional* effort of remarkable vigour.'[1]

De Tocqueville was judging the USA from the perspectives of the relatively more mature countries of Western Europe; and, in a sense, a similar anxiety, mixed with distrust, is often noticeable today in the evaluation of the non-Western world by more mature nations.

While de Tocqueville spoke of the need to build a new political society which could sustain democratic institutions, later scholars have heavily underlined the correlationship between industrialisation and urbanisation, on the one hand, and democratic institutions and their continued stability, on the other. Karl de Schweinitz in *Industrialisation and Democracy* (1964) heavily underlined the relationship between 'economic growth' and 'democracy'. He maintained that the industrial revolution of the second half of the eighteenth century in Britain and America accelerated the rate of economic development and brought in its wake profound social and economic changes which 'could not be accommodated within the oligarchic institutions bequeathed to Britain in the Glorious Revolution'.[2]

In particular the growing wealth of the middle class, the concentration of the labour force in urban areas and the growth of population created an irresistible demand on the part of the unenfranchised to be admitted into 'the pale of the constitution'.

While the economic forces were seen by de Schweinitz as the causal forces – creating new conditions and bringing about changes within the political system – historically speaking, within such a cause and effect situation specific countries follow specific routes, which are never again repeated:

> One thing, however, emerges clearly . . . the development of democracy in the nineteenth century was a function of an unusual configuration of historical circumstances which cannot be repeated. The Euro-American route to democracy is closed. Other means must now be devised for building new democratic states.[3]

To de Schweinitz, 'chance' has played an important part in the building of democratic institutions in the Western world; as, for instance, in Britain, where they were the unintended end-product of a series of social and economic events.[4]

Barrington Moore, Jr, in his *Social Origins of Dictatorship and Democracy* (1967), has pointed out the variations in the resultant political institutions of the countries of Europe, America and Asia when they became industrialised. To Moore, two sets of actors, namely the landed upper class and the peasantry, by means of a variety of efforts towards economic modernisation, produced political institutions ranging from bourgeois democracy to communism.

From Lipset and Lerner down to Huntington the growth of political participation has often been considered to be a function of economic development and/or urbanisation. In *Political Man* (1959) Lipset argued that there was a positive correlation between economic development and stable political democracy,[5] and his thesis on the congruence of the two was subsequently worked out by Philips Cutright in terms of the 'relatedness' of societal forces.[6] Earlier, in an influential paper, Daniel Lerner came out with a model which identified urbanisation as a critical factor which gave rise to literacy, the growth of the media, industrial technology and, finally, the 'institutions of participation'.[7] In treating urbanisation as a prime mover Lerner was seeking universal validity for what was essentially a Western experience. Most recently, in *No Easy Choice: Political Participation in Developing Countries* (1976), Samuel Huntington and Joan Nelson point out: 'The expansion of political participation is found to be more the byproduct of socioeconomic modernization than conscious first-choice of individuals, groups, or elite.'[8]

But in the case of India the constitutional provision for political participation *was* the conscious first choice of the founders of the Indian republic. They made provision for it in advance of the economic modernisation of society. In fact it was their hope that public participation itself would play a major role in economic development and social change in general.

The Indian national movement had primarily focused its demand on responsible government based on universal adult suffrage. Such a demand was largely due to the assimilation of Western liberal ideology by the political elite and the pattern of withdrawal by the British *Raj* from the Indian sub-continent. Britain introduced responsible government and the widening of franchise incrementally and grudgingly. It was then left to the nationalist leaders, when they assumed power after independence, to provide for unrestricted political participation in constituting political authority at the federal and state levels.

The growth of political participation in India, in other words, was not a function of economic development or urbanisation. In fact its introduction without them was an act of faith on the part of her founding fathers. They believed that the average Indian ought to be involved in the challenge and excitement of building a new society. Jawaharlal Nehru even maintained that unless the average man was involved, sufficient momentum would not be generated to allow the colossal task of nation-building and economic development to be undertaken.

Political participation in India was largely a product of history, and an ideological commitment on the part of a generation of nationalist leaders who discovered its special significance to her hierarchically ordered social organisation and traditionally submissive attitude to political authority. The commitment to liberal ideology on the part of the nationalist leaders did not stop at the initial introduction of universal adult suffrage in the euphoric years following independence. In the following decade it was further extended to the constitution of political authority at the village, sub-district, and district levels and also towards routing the entire development process through them.

Such faith in political participation on the part of the founding fathers might have been misplaced so far as its capacity to help solve the enormous problems of the economy in the shortest possible time was concerned. Nevertheless, it did prove to be a powerful force in overcoming the constraints imposed by primary groups and building a secular participatory society on the one hand, and in reversing the trends towards authoritarianism at the most critical period in her history, on the other.

I THE PROBLEM

The individual is born to ethnicity, makes his living, by and large, in the class of his birth, and shares the perspectives of his generation. None the less, electoral processes, party organisations, mass movements and the search for better economic returns induce or force him to take up a position and make secular decisions on issues which lie outside the primary groups to which he belongs. While he continues to live his social life within the primary groups to which he was born, the constraints imposed by such groups, on his thinking and movement, tend to become increasingly weaker in the face of his need to act effectively in conjunction with others. Cumulatively, the rationale for his secular decisions and activity in concert with others establishes a new pattern of behaviour which undergoes changes when he is faced with new challenges.

Each developing society struggling to modernise itself politically registers its own peculiar, complex, and often internally self-contradictory, processes. And to go in search of their 'evolutionary universals',[9] to use Talcott Parsons's phrase, in advance of sufficient knowledge of those processes, may in the end prove to be a barren exercise.

Ever since Lipset, in *Political Man*, wrote about the indispensability to democracy of party organisations, unions and interest associations based on cross-cutting ethnic and religious ties, political scientists and anthropologists studying political development have paid much attention to the problem of the use of social cohesion in electoral and administrative matters. Throughout the 1950s and 1960s, for instance, the bulk of studies on Indian politics concentrated heavily on the nagging question of ethnic, religious and linguistic cohesion and the need to cut across them for enduring national integration and healthy democratic development.

With a few exceptions, from the very beginning, party organisations in democratic India have had a base of support that cuts
across regional sentiment and ethnic and religious ties. This is
because the horizontal dispersal of caste groups, further sub-divided
by the sentiment of village, lineage and kin group neighbourhood,
compelled the competing party organisations to build support
structures for themselves across their divisions. Furthermore, the
boundaries of electoral constituencies did not coincide with the
boundaries of these groups. The party organisations gave electoral
identity to the constituencies, frequently associated the names of
certain candidates with them, and also nursed them for the periodic
elections. For them the base of support was not just something out
there, waiting to be picked up. They had to carve it out across
divisions of all kinds.

In that respect the party organisations in India were no different
from their counterparts in plural societies such as those of the
United States, Canada, Belgium and Holland. They all build a
patchwork of support structures across ethnic, religious and linguistic divisions. Where the Indian experience differed from that of
Western democracies was in the fact that, so far as social
organisation was concerned, the ethnic groups in the former stood in
a hierarchical relationship. And to the extent to which the
hierarchical element also indicated a corresponding difference in
economic, political and educational attainments, the lower strata in
particular were severely handicapped in their exercise of electoral
choice. But, as this study will show, despite their manifold
disadvantages, the lower strata, over the years, also began to catch
up with their social superiors in matters relating to the search for
political alternatives.

During the three decades of democratic experience what was clearly
identifiable in rural areas and their urban periphery was the
phenomenal rise to power of the agriculturists, who occupied a
middle caste position in the traditional social organisation. With
their existing economic base, they either increased their land-
holding, entered into trade and commerce, started small industrial
units, or, with their well-knit extended family, proliferated into all
these areas of economic activity. Economically as well as ethnically
this was the group that surged forward. Its 'middle' position in the
social hierarchy did not worry it for long and through a substantial
increase in economic standing and political power it even tried to

enhance its social standing within the traditional organisation.

The approach to economic advancement and political power, or indeed the use of the latter to obtain the former, proved to be far more complex in the case of the lower strata of society. The introduction of democratic institutions and procedures gave them the potential for political power before they could secure an economic base for its effective use. Moreover, in the beginning they used their newly acquired political power to overcome the social humiliation which the hierarchically ordered social organisation had imposed upon them; and only subsequently used it to demand improvement of their economic condition.

The initial demand for temple entry by the ex-untouchables of India rather than for economic relief on a massive scale resembled the demand for common buses by Blacks in the southern United States and the demand by the East Africans after independence for entry into the hotels and clubs from which they had been excluded. The demands of the ex-untouchables for education, jobs, housing and other facilities followed only after the old scores had been settled with their erstwhile superiors. For social as well as historical reasons, therefore, different segments within developing as well as developed societies are able to make only unequal use of their newly acquired political power.

In traditional India social hierarchy was popularised, by the upper strata, as a desirable norm. Its maintenance became a moral obligation on the part of the rulers. Such a past left deep scars of humiliation on the lower strata of traditional Hindu society. Obsession with social humiliation, and the consequent drive to improve social status, even in democratic India, has been in direct proportion to one's place in the hierarchically ordered social organisation.

Three decades of democratic experience, with intensely contested local, state and national elections, have socialised the Indians, regardless of their position in the social hierarchy, into a *common* political citizenship across the traditional divides. But the extension of such a citizenship into the economic field whereby irrespective of his place in the social hierarchy, an individual would be able to claim the right to economic advancement and distributive justice, has yet to take place. While the right to vote was granted by the Indian constitution, the realisation of economic demands requires unionised or collective pressure with or without the support of political parties. So far, barring the urban centres and industrial areas, the lower-income groups, dispersed in rural areas, have not been able even to formulate their demands, let alone generate pressures for their realisation. The national as well as state governments have been able to get away with electoral promises, 'blueprints', unimplemented legislation and the formal ideology of socialism.

In fact awareness on the part of the poorer segments of society regarding the possible use of their newly acquired political power to improve their economic condition has taken much longer to evolve. Initially they merely used it to become the equals of their traditional social superiors. The slur and the stigma of being considered *neech* (low) or socially inferior and/or of criminal disposition, devoid of human dignity, loomed large in their thinking, enough to use up several years of possible political action that might have been directed towards their economic improvement.

The movement towards a fair deal for the poor and their social rehabilitation was stimulated by the sense of guilt on the part of the liberals. As the lower segments assimilated a few gains, their consciousness and expectations increased.

The main thrust for social change, to give them a better deal, did not come from the poor segments themselves. From Karl Marx to Barrington Moore, attempts have been made to understand this enigma. The vertical divisions within the social organisation reinforced by the horizontal divisions of dispersed rural communities were often identified as the main obstacles to the poor and the needy generating enough political pressure to support their demands. However, over the last three decades, civil administration, a vastly expanded public transport system, the spread of literacy, the newspapers, economic planning and electioneering activity by the party organisations have together successfully penetrated through the barriers and identified the major problems. What has yet to emerge, as we shall see in this study, is the common identity, consciousness and political will – the three major elements Marx underlined for effective class conflict – on the part of the poorer strata of Indian society.

In developing countries it is often easier to work up the emotions of the masses against the alien rule or towards the restoration of democratic rights already enjoyed than in support of the economic demands of the non-unionised poor. Nevertheless, the moral commitment of the bulk of the political elite, the party platforms and electoral promises and the increasingly questioning attitude of the electorate may create the necessary conditions for building up such support. In India social legislation for a better deal for the rural and urban poor has already been put on the statute book. But so far it has been counter-productive. However, if the competing political parties could be persuaded that to produce the intended results of such legislation would in the end strengthen their own bases of political power, they would be much more interested in implementing it. In all this an active and demanding electorate has a great role to play.

One of the interesting questions to raise, especially in connection with those countries which attained their independence two or three decades ago, is whether there has been persistence or a shift in the generation that has attained independence, manned major state institutions, involved itself in the consolidation of independence, and made decisions of far-reaching importance. Such a time-span makes the question worth while.

This study will examine the question not in terms of persistence or shift but with regard to the co-existence of generations: bringing into play a clash of perspectives, of norms of conduct in public life, of identification of issues, and the extent of tolerance of political expediencies.

Party organisations in developing societies occupy a peculiar position. They mobilise the individual out of his primary groups by involving him in the democratic process. At the same time, however, they themselves are influenced, to some extent, especially in between electoral contests, by the manner in which individuals in such groups transact their business.

In the literature on party organisations an inordinate emphasis has been put on their 'interest aggregation' function. It has heavily underlined the fact that the main function of party organisations is to engage in 'linkage' activity of the citizenry with the political system. That indeed would be the case if we were to deduce the functions of party organisations from what they do during the periods preceding elections. But such periods are short-lived. It is important, therefore, to examine also what they do between elections.

Office-bearers, activists and marginals engage in linkage activity on behalf of political parties particularly during the periods preceding elections. But in between elections, as we shall see, they do not always work towards the persistence of the linkage structure at all levels of party operation. At times they even get involved in activity and issues which erode the laboriously built party support structure.

Such paradoxical behaviour on the part of the linkmen, in a sense, is inherent in the situation of party strife where cleavages for electoral contests are formed across the primary groups. Between elections, the activists and marginals enjoy a wide range of political flexibility. During such periods, they often enter into political alignments across the party fence. Unlike office-bearers they do not don party uniform all the time and when the electoral thunder and rhetoric dies down they enter into political dialogue across the party divide.

The situation is, then, as this study will point out, one of building the patchwork of support for electoral strife and then dismantling it for inter-party accommodations. Post-election periods, in particular, are often conducive to the resumption of normal sociability across the party barrier and along the lines of ethnicity, class, generations and their possible combinations.

It is necessary now to examine some of the peculiarities of India's emerging political society. In order to sustain democratic institutions and procedures, every country needs a political society which shares its underlying values and manifests commitment to them in its political activity.

The political society of India, which has sustained her democratic institutions, has been in the making for nearly a century. Her prolonged struggle for freedom, the dedication and calibre of her nationalist leaders, and above all their deep commitment to democratic values, have firmly laid the foundation of her new political society.

Such a foundation was later on firmed up by the political mobilisation of her socially cohesive groups. As they went through the democratic process, they learned to make a distinction between the area of their primary social concern and that of secular democratic politics. Such a bifurcation in the economic field, making a distinction between the occupation of one's birth and the secular collectivity of interest groups to protect one's interests, has yet to emerge on a widespread scale.

Within the political society, the mobilisation of the masses soon became a two-way process: of marshalling support for party organisations and of seeking accountability for performance and results especially from those who were in power.

Some aspects of political society, reflecting a widespread belief in certain basic political values, also emerged; namely: that political authority could be constituted only by means of elections; that change of government had to be peaceful; that the political zero-sum-game had to be discouraged; and that the due processes of law were not to be abrogated under any circumstances. There also emerged an unresolved contradiction indicating a longing for administrative firmness without wanting to give up any of the hard-won civil liberties.

Let us now briefly summarise the problem this study will examine. The question of ethnic cohesion is of fundamental importance in understanding the nature of the democratic process in India. This is because, in order to make the exercise of political choice possible, the democratic process has to make inroads into certain areas of ethnic cohesion. The question is to what extent and by what means the democratic institutions secured the conditions whereby electoral differentiations within all segments of Indian society become possible.

Closely connected with this is the question of the use of political power by the different strata of society. For social as well as historical reasons not all of them were able initially to direct its use towards their basic economic problems. The question is, what explains such an unequal use of power and whether there is evidence of its possible wider use, particularly by the lower strata of society, in the future.

Along with these questions we shall also examine the part played by generational differences in influencing perspectives, accepted norms and the perception of issues; the process of strife and accommodation which party organisations engage in; and the emergence of a political society, indicative of a growing political capacity, which can sustain democratic institutions.

We shall examine these questions against the background of theoretical controversies and empirical data which I collected in an urban community in western India called Anand. The study of Anand also includes the adjoining town of Vidyanagar, which is the seat of a university. For the purposes of our research the twin towns were considered as one – Anand.

II THE METHOD

As has already been said, this study is largely based on field-work in the urban community of Anand, spread over the eleven years 1966–77. During that period a large number of people were interviewed repeatedly. Among them a stratified sample of 500 voters, which was later on increased to 600, was interviewed ten times. The reason for interviewing the *same* people again and again over an extended period of time was to understand, as realistically as possible, the nature and extent of their involvement in the democratic process, given all the constraints of a developing society.

The democratic process in a developing country like India, with the complexities of her social structure, economic disparity and traditional attitude to authority, cannot be satisfactorily examined within a short time-span. The involvement of the people in the process and the consequent changes in their attitude to elected deputies, public policy and its implementation, all call for continuing examination. The democratic process is about people in their role as citizens and electorate, and such a role becomes increasingly complex when they grow in their political capacity. The growth of such a capacity needs to be examined in terms of its sequence and efficacy. Most social scientists studying developing societies are unable to spend sufficient time observing the complexities of their transition. In the words of Professor Samuel Eldersveld:

> Unfortunately most of our research on developing societies is not 'developmental'. That is, if there is empirical research at all, it consists primarily of research at one point in time. What is needed is sound 'historical' or 'longitudinal' analysis which permits generalisation about the society at various stages of its development, and which is able to determine the extent to which the society is moving towards political or social or economic goal.[10]

There are other reasons why a longitudinal analysis of the democratic process in India becomes indispensable. Among the developing countries, India gave rise to a peculiar situation by holding on to her democratic institutions. And she has done this in advance of her economic modernisation. She even genuinely believes that through democratic means she will be able to attain the twin goals of economic development and social and economic equality. This, then, further adds to the complexity of studying her democratic process. But the greatest difficulty lies in the inadequacy of the theoretical tools available in the social sciences for understanding such societies. The corpus of theoretical knowledge has developed in advance of, or even irrespective of, the peculiar problems which such societies present. This inadequacy of knowledge often blinkers inquiry or starts from assumptions which are not warranted. It takes a continuing observation of a phenomenon to be able to question the adequacy of the conceptual tools themselves. In particular this volume will illustrate the varying degree of inadequacy of the concepts of social cohesion, class, linkage, and democratic process in general.

For its analysis this study deliberately draws a narrow circle. While the problems that it examines are often related to the main currents of theoretical knowledge, and its general arguments are also formulated within the framework of competing explanations, the basic understanding of the democratic process is arrived at by concentrating on its complexities in an urban, and, to some extent, a rural community.

Neither the urban nor the rural community referred to in this volume are representative of other communities. In fact no community, rural or urban, *can* be representative of other communities. What has been attempted here instead is the identification of the *phenomenon* of the democratic process within the traditional constraints of hierarchy, poverty and a submissive attitude to authority. The understanding of such a phenomenon can be valid elsewhere provided its implicit assertions are subjected to rigorous empirical tests in different situations. And even if it is not valid elsewhere, it certainly can become a useful starting-point for exploring significant differences. After all, the most incisive statement on the democratic process in the United States also came out of an intensive study of a community, namely New Haven, at the hands of Robert Dahl.

Both a specific study like the present one, and a study that bases its generalisations on watered-down national aggregates, will create a feeling of dissatisfaction.[11] Social scientists have yet to produce a satisfactory integration of the two approaches. Approaches which rely on unintegrated combinations of the two offer conflicting perspectives and have methodological problems of their own.

Consequently, one is often forced to choose between the more reliable and meaningful insight which an intensive study of a limited area brings, and the fairly general picture, often lacking in concreteness, which an extensive study provides. Nevertheless, whatever the scale of one's research, in the final analysis, one has to *deduce* inferences, explanations and general arguments from whatever one has observed, so as to be able to formulate one's theoretical generalisations. In either case, by means of generalisations what is sought is the extension of the validity of one's findings from an area that is more familiar to an area that is less familiar. And in each case, again, one leaves it to the community of scholars to scrutinise, reinforce or refute the validity of such extensions. In other words, such claims do not become valid simply because one has taken into account a narrower or a wider area of study, but because one's fellow scientists have also subjected such claims to their own tests and scrutiny and have found them valid.

Anand is a rapidly industrialising, middle-sized town (population about 100,000 in 1977) in western India. In 1966 its electoral roll consisted of 24,357 voters. My research team first of all identified the sub-caste and religion of the voters. The names of these voters were then reserialised into 34 sub-caste, religious and linguistic categories.[12] To be able to draw a stratified random sample of 500 voters, every fiftieth name was picked up. Five years later, in 1971, a group of 50 first-time voters was added, and in 1975 a further 50 first-time voters were included. That brought the total number in our sample to 600.

During 1966–7, the voters in our sample were interviewed three times: twice before the General Election of 1967, and once after. The sample of voters was interviewed twice again in 1971: before and after the General Election. During the Assembly election of 1972, the voters in the sample were interviewed twice again: before and after the election. The same was repeated in the Assembly election of 1975. Finally, in 1977, owing to the then prevailing atmosphere of fear under the emergency rule, less than half the number of voters in the sample could be interviewed before the election.[13]

Despite the fact that most of the interviews were conducted before and after elections, this study is not, in a strict sense, about voting behaviour. It is, on the other hand, a study of the role of the party organisations, elite, interest groups, etc., in mobilising the electorate out of the traditional cohesive groups to which they were born, into a political society where decisions on political and economic matters affecting everyone, regardless of social origin, are made. As a longitudinal study it seeks to identify the shrinking area of social cohesion to its primary social concerns, and the expanding area of political society where people born to different ethnic and occupational classes and generations are able to come together to build secular collectivities to pursue their common political and economic goals. Against such a background I have sought to identify the emergence, characteristics and some of the inherent contradictions of the new political society in India which, despite a few crises, has been able to sustain and strengthen her democratic institutions.

In this study, the factors of ethnicity, class and generation are not treated as variables, dependent or independent, for a correlational or causal analysis. The complexity of cohesion which each provides, and its gradual retraction in the face of the emergence of a new political society, are not susceptible to analysis, correlational or causal, with the help of discrete and cut-and-dried variables. In political development studies an analysis of such a transition was attempted by Daniel Lerner[14], and led to interminable controversy. Lerner had argued that democratic political participation had followed urbanisation and other social forces which it stimulated. The question was whether urbanisation and other forces stood in a correlational or causal relationship with the growth of democratic institutions. Despite the empirical studies undertaken, with a number of highly sophisticated methodologies, to support and oppose Lerner's theory, the controversy remained inconclusive.[15]

This study has also advisedly left out the question of education or literacy, for two reasons. First, there is the widespread fallacy which equates formal literacy with *political* literacy. In fact, one has little to do with the other. It was because of such a fallacy that a number of reporters, both inside and outside India, expressed great surprise when the formally illiterate electorate of India displayed extraordinary *political* literacy in throwing out the Congress Party from office in the historic General Election of 1977. That election had nothing to do with literacy in a formal sense. What it had displayed, on the other hand, was the growing political capacity, discrimination and courage on the part of the Indian electorate. Second, in a longitudinal study of this nature, how very precisely can one identify the element of literacy or education over a decade in the same people? Like the experiences of life, the involvement in the democratic process itself created conditions for continuing political education.

III   THE COMMUNITY

In 1966, when we began our field-work in Anand, its population was around 60,000. By the time we completed our work in 1977, its population had risen to nearly 100,000. Its extraordinary commercial, industrial and educational development had attracted the unemployed rural poor, as well as businessmen, industrialists, skilled and semi-skilled people, doctors, lawyers, teachers, managers and technocrats. During the last half-century Anand came to be known for its various achievements: as a centre of medical facilities, for its grain trade, its medium-scale industries, its educational facilities and above all as the focus for Asia's largest milk co-operative dairy, AMUL. To social scientists, however, its greatest attraction lies in its active citizenry, a highly politicised middle-class and a political elite which believed in building a viable political opposition to the Congress Party from the time democracy was first introduced in India.

Two aspects of Anand may provide a useful background to our analysis of the political process there: its ethnic composition and its institutions. We shall now examine each of these in some detail.

ETHNIC ANAND

(a)   The Brahmins
Anand had witnessed the rise and fall in political importance of many ethnic groups, including the Brahmins. In the late eighteenth century, they started settling in various near-by villages and although they established the village of Anand, they did not move into it till a suitable economic opportunity presented itself. Their priestly work had furnished them with liquid cash which was to prove very useful when the time came. With the help of surplus cash they not only bought large tracts of land but also entered into the business of money-lending. The Brahmins who settled in Anand and constituted 7 per cent of its population were known as the Bajkhedawal. Then there were other segments among them.

At the time of the advent of the Brahmins in Anand the bulk of the land belonged to the Patidars. The Patidars, because of their extravagant spending on marriage and death ceremonies, were always short of cash. They therefore started selling portions of their land to the Brahmins.

Income from land, money-lending, traditional priestly occupation, and also small-scale commerce, furnished the Brahmins of Anand with a sound economic base. To this were added the other two factors which helped them to wrench political power from the Patidars. In the Indian Mutiny of 1857 some Patidars had played an active part. This led to reprisals by the British against the entire Patidar community. The British officials often excluded Patidars from administrative positions and gave them to the Brahmins. Moreover, during the second half of the nineteenth century, the British administration had penetrated deeper into the district. It therefore needed additional administrative personnel with some education. That, too, favoured the Brahmins.

The Brahmins entered politics via the municipality. In 1884, the Bombay Municipal Act made Anand a municipality. The municipal board had two categories of members: official and non-official. Up to the First World War, the Brahmins dominated the municipality. After that the Patidars, who had staged an economic recovery, took over.

At the top leadership level there continued to be a few clashes but these did not develop into politically significant cleavages between the Brahmins and Patidars. The various cleavage structures in the governing bodies of the major institutions in Anand in fact cut across their ethnic groups. This was partly due to the fact that neither the Brahmins nor the Patidars were socially homogeneous groups. But that was not the only reason for the lack of political homogeneity among them. Diversity of occupation, the effect of influential people in the residential areas, and above all individual perception of political issues, had succeeded in splitting the Brahmin as well as the Patidar vote in all the elections of Anand.

Being essentially a middle-class group, the Brahmins of Anand were badly hit by the phenomenal rise in the cost of living. Consequently, they became most critical of Congress politics. While the bulk of the Brahmins wanted to find an alternative to the Congress Party, those among them who worked in various public enterprises felt compelled to support it.

(b)   The Banias

The Banias of Anand made up about 5 per cent of Anand's population but, due to their sound economic base, they wielded political influence which was quite disproportionate to their

number. Like the Brahmins, the Banias, too, were an unhomo-
geneous group. The phenomenal growth of the grain trade in
Anand together with the highly expanded scope for money-lending
and commerce had attracted the Banias to Anand from different
parts of Gujarat. In all social matters, however, they continued to
retain strong ties with the villages from which they had come.

Unable to break the hold of the Patidars on the wide range of
economic activity in Anand as well as in the district, the Banias
realised that their economic future lay in good relations with the
Patidars.

The Banias were highly critical of the policies of the Congress
Party, which put great restrictions on their economic activity. They
strongly believed in the unrestricted operation of the market
economy and claimed that whenever the state encroached upon
economic activity it spelt disaster. A prominent Bania businessman
repeated the well-known saying in Gujarati,

'Jyan Raja bane Vepari
Tyan Praja bane Bhikari'.
(In the country where the king takes on the role of businessman,
the people will become beggars.)

Under Congress rule, the Banias maintained, the goal of
improving the lot of the common man had remained merely a
slogan. What the Congress Party in fact did was to favour the group
of businessmen who supported it and to put restrictions on those
who opposed it.

(c)   The Patidars
This brings us to the politically most important community of
Anand, and indeed of the state of Gujarat: the Patidars. They
constituted just under a quarter of Anand's population and its
second largest social group. They dominated Anand's trade and
commerce, industry, banking, transport, educational institutions,
middle-class professions and party organisations. The district of
Kaira, where Anand is located, owed much to their boundless
energy, innovative spirit and pragmatic outlook. Whatever the
form of economic activity – agriculture, commerce, industry – the
Patidars of the district were always on top of it. Similarly, whatever
the party organisation, ideology or movement, the Patidars were
there either to champion it or to oppose it.

Unlike the Brahmins and Banias, the status of the Patidars within
the social organisation was a matter of controversy and unparalleled
mobility. Until the end of the nineteenth century, the Patidars were
identified in the British records as the *Kanbis*[16] (agriculturists). Some
Gujarati writers even classified them as *Vaishyas* (merchants), *Sudras*
(lower caste), and *Kshatriyas* (warrior caste).[17]

According to M. N. Srinivas, in the past for some castes, the
Indian census offered one of their rare opportunities for social
mobility.[18] As far as the Patidars were concerned, they succeeded in
including Patel rather than Kanabi as their caste surname in the
census records. Furthermore, when the Bombay Government in
1928 decided to classify the Hindu society into upper, middle and
lower segments, the Patidars once again succeeded in getting their
claim as upper caste Hindus recognised.[19]

The social mobility of the Patidars, however, was chiefly made
possible by certain economic and political changes during the past
150 years in this region. For one thing, the peculiarity of the land-
tenure system during the pre-British days helped them to enter into
the revenue bureaucracy.[20] From such a vantage point, an increase
in their land-holding and entry into the power structure was most
natural.

Since the turn of the century, the Patidars have registered greater
social mobility than any other social group in Gujarat. They have
successfully used their continually improving economic base,
administrative experience and political power to attain higher
social status. As a social group, however, the Patidars themselves are
not free from internal hierarchies, which to some extent induce
them to go in search of higher social recognition within their own
group. These hierarchies are of two different strands: the hierarchy
which arose as a result of Patidar induction into the revenue
bureaucracy of the pre-British period; and the hierarchy which
crystallised out of the claims of the six *mota gams* (prestigious
villages) of the Patidars in the district.

The Patidars who performed administrative functions in the pre-
British days came to be known as *Amins*.[21] Then there were *Desais*
who had acted as revenue contractors in the past, and who adopted
Desai as their surname. The Amins and Desais, because of their
administrative background, considered themselves to be a cut
above the average Patidar. They did not, however, become an
endogamous group.

The other hierarchy arose from the attempt by the six *mota gams* –

Sojitra, Dharmaj, Karamsad, Nadiad, Bhadaran and Vaso – to constitute themselves into a circle of marriage. Some of these villages are very old and it is said that reference to Sojitra, in particular, as Sojitrus,[22] is to be found even in classical Greek literature.

The Patidars of the *mota gams* were the first to undergo Western education and become receptive to new ideas. While the Patidars of other villages were mostly pursuing agriculture until Indian independence, the sons of the *mota gams* were making a great name for themselves as doctors, engineers, lawyers, administrators, businessmen and industrialists. Although initially they had added the dimension of *achievement*, in order to gain permanent advantage from it, they banded themselves into an exclusive matrimonial group called the *gol*. If someone from outside this *gol* wanted to marry his daughter to a male in these prestigious villages, he was required to pay an inordinate amount of cash and jewellery by way of a dowry.

In effect such a hypergamous arrangement, whereby a non-*mota gam* Patidar worked hard and with cash obtained himself a *mota gam* son-in-law, raised his status within his own matrimonial circle. For the industrious Patidar, the *mota gams* performed the function of an aristocracy to which only the daughters of affluent Patidars could be admitted. David Pocock has appropriately described the Patidar hypergamy as a 'free hypergamy', whereby the restriction on marrying above one's class could be overcome by means of a dowry.[23]

The consolidation of the *mota gams* into a matrimonial circle had a far-reaching effect on other villages of the Patidars. They, too, now wanted to institutionalise the area of their matrimonial circle or *gols*.

The Patidars of Anand belong to a *gol* of their own called the *moti satyavis*. Its leading commercial and industrial elite has partly come from *nani satyavis*. And so far as the *mota gam* Patidars in Anand are concerned, with the exception of a few, the bulk of them are in middle-class professions. Such a divergence between their social status and economic standing often causes tensions among them. So far as achievements in terms of commerce, industry, education and American-degree-holding children are concerned, the Patidars of the *mota gams* have been clearly excelled by the others.

The point to be emphasised here is two-fold. First, the Patidars on the governing bodies of various institutions would sometimes enter into curious political accommodations with others across the party fence provided they happened to be of the same *gols*. We shall illustrate this in the chapter on party organisation. And, second, the Patidars, having attained a relatively higher social status of their own, were not obsessed, like the Kshatriyas, with the problem of social standing within the Hindu social organisation. That gave them a free hand to use their political power to attain other goals.

At the turn of the century the leading men of the Patidars in the district began to emphasise the need for education. That led to the opening of a number of schools and the establishment of the *Charotar Education Society*, run by dedicated teachers. This body, as we shall see later on, exercised great influence on the district. By 1901, Anand became a railway junction connecting trains to Ahmedabad in the north, Baroda and Bombay in the south, Godhara in the east and Cambay in the west.

The railways opened up distant markets for the agricultural products of Anand and its district. They also stimulated the cultivation of cotton, tobacco, and the growth of the grain trade in Anand. By the end of the Second World War, Anand had become a leading grain centre in western India. The Patidars were mainly responsible for the growth of agriculture and commerce during this period.

The Patidars of Anand were deeply involved in the national movement for independence. Almost all the leaders who were active in the national movement were also deeply involved in the educational and social reform movement.

They vigorously participated in all the elections in Anand. From 1957 onwards, their vote was highly differentiated. From 1962 onwards, a large number of Patidars actively went in search of a political alternative to the Congress Party. Being a hardworking people themselves, they disliked the Congress philosophy of welfare provisions through high taxes.

(d) The Kshatriyas

In all the elections in Anand it was often heard said, that a candidate had a good chance of winning if the Kshatriyas supported him, for they constituted the largest composite social group, comprising a quarter of Anand's total population. The Kshatriyas were a group of clans, some more closely knit than others, with rigid endogamous networks which linked them to 242 different villages in the region for marriage and ritual observances. Among them the clans of Chauhans, Chavadas, Gohels, Thakores, and Parmars stood in a hierarchical relation with one another. There were few Chauhans, but they stood above the rest. The Chavadas and Gohels had an equal status and the Thakurs were considered to be the outsiders. The status of the Parmars remained a matter of dispute.

The exact position of the Kshatriyas within the Hindu social organisation has remained a matter of controversy among the historians and anthropologists, with the genealogists taking yet another position. Like the Patidars, though not as much, the Kshatriyas too have registered some degree of social mobility.

With the Patidars, the search for new social identity within the Hindu social organisation – because of their high rate of economic development, political power and relatively few internal differences – did not become an issue of great importance. But it did as far as the Kshatriyas were concerned. For the rank and file, recognition *as* a Kshatriya in the 1950s and 1960s in the emerging political society of India was as important as the problem of political participation or a better standard of living. The more a Kshatriya asserted his identity the more he became aware of the social distance between him and the upper-crust Rajputs, and the other higher groups in the social organisation. Despite attempts at 'homogenisation'[24] of the Kshatriya community as a whole, as we shall see later on, deeply entrenched social hierarchy continued. What finally helped the Kshatriyas to shed their sense of social inferiority to some extent was their involvement in the democratic process itself. Through it they were able to circumvent, at least in the political field, the disadvantages of their socially inferior position.

Economically speaking, the Kshatriyas of Anand were a backward group. They made a living as small-scale agriculturists and unskilled workers, or by doing odd jobs. In recent years some of them learned some trades and were employed as semi-skilled and skilled workers in the industrial units of Anand.

With the introduction of universal adult suffrage, the Kshatriyas of the constituency became the most important single factor in democratic politics. In the first two General Elections, the Congress Party had no difficulty in mobilising them in its favour. By putting the Land Tenancy Act, which promised land to the tenants, on the statute book and by an incessant talk of socialism, the Congress Party had acquired a pro-underdog image for itself. Consequently, during the elections of 1952 and 1957, it had no difficulty in getting the near unanimous support of the Kshatriyas. But in 1962, a great

problem was created for the Kshatriyas when their caste association, the Kshatriya Sabha (Sabha), dominated by feudal elements
and princes, asked them to vote for the Swatantra Party instead.
Despite such a directive, four-fifths of the Kshatriyas continued to
support the Congress Party.

The District Congress Party was quick to realise this mood of the
Kshatriyas. It encouraged their leaders of humble birth to form a
rival association, namely the Kshatriya Samaj (Samaj). The Samaj
was considered to be an organisation of the poor Kshatriyas, and,
while some upper-crust Rajputs sided with it, they were not elected
to any of the official positions. It played an important part in getting
a Kshatriya of humble birth elected as a member of the Legislative
Assembly of Gujarat in 1967. In subsequent elections neither the
Sabha nor the Samaj played a significant role.

For nearly three decades, the Congress Party had enjoyed
Kshatriya support, largely due to its pro-poor image. Over the years
the support for it among the Kshatriyas started declining owing to
its failure to produce the promised results. But, unlike the
economically self-reliant Patidars, the Kshatriyas depended a great
deal on state policy and its consequences for their well-being. Such a
dependence inhibited their search for political alternatives to the
Congress Party.

(e) The Christians
The Christians of Anand were divided into three categories: the
Catholics; the followers of the Salvation Army (Mukti Foj); and the
followers of the Irish Presbyterian Mission. While the Catholics
were the first to establish themselves in the vicinity, the Salvation
Army, because of its excellent medical facilities, was able to build a
much broader base in Anand. Together they constituted 4 per cent
of Anand's population.

In 1910, the Salvation Army founded what is known as the
Amery Hospital near Anand railway station. The hospital attracted
highly qualified and dedicated doctors from different parts of the
world. During the years 1923–44 it was served by a gifted surgeon
from New Zealand called Bramwell Cook. He attracted patients
from as far as Ahmedabad and Bombay. When he retired, the
people of Anand wrote a volume in his honour entitled *The White
Gujarati*. Because of his surgical talents, Anand came to be
recognised as the medical centre for the region.

The organisers of the Salvation Army and the Catholic Mission put a great emphasis on education and helped their people to get employment in various institutions and industries. The Catholics in particular organised industries and ran a highly modern press called the Anand Printing Press. The Irish Mission did not have much success in Anand. The hospital it ran closed down after nearly two decades of service.

The Christians of Anand were most impressed by the Congress Party under Nehru wanting to build a secular India in which her people would enjoy freedom of conscience. In less than a decade after independence, especially for the Christians, secularism ceased to be an election issue. Consequently, from 1962 onwards, the votes of the Christians became increasingly differentiated.

(f) The Muslims

The Muslims of Anand constituted about 8 per cent of Anand's population. All the major four divisions among the Muslims – namely, Sheikhs, Syeds, Moghuls, and Pathans – were represented there. But there were others also: a sizeable group of Vohras, who were mostly shopkeepers, and Sipahis (watchman), Molesalams (landowners), Maleks (shopkeepers and cultivators), Tais and Momnas (weavers) and Chunars (bricklayers).[25]

Since the partition of India, the Muslims of Anand had stayed away from the mainstream of its political life. Even the educated or the economically prosperous among them did not think in terms of entering into civic or regional politics. Some of them chose to act as brokers between civic politicians and Muslim voters so as to be able to get permits and licences for business for themselves.

For a long time the Congress Party had succeeded in exploiting the Muslims' sense of insecurity. Directly or indirectly they were told that under a non-Congress regime their freedom of conscience would be seriously threatened. Paradoxically, by declaring itself secular, the Congress Party had secured the benefit of votes of all those religious minority communities which felt threatened for real or imaginary reasons.

By the 1960s, however, the Congress strategy began to run out its course. Increasingly, the Muslims began to feel assured of the secular future of India no matter which political party came to power. The Vohras, as we shall see, were the first to diversify their votes. The others followed, though not in large numbers. Whenever communal riots broke out in any part of India, the process of diversification of the Muslim votes received a serious setback.

During the period of emergency and in the election of 1977, Mrs Gandhi in particular pinned her hopes on Muslim votes. But the excesses of the sterilisation programme and the forcible eviction of Muslims in certain parts of Delhi reported in the newspapers, forced the Muslims to reappraise their electoral loyalty to the Congress Party. In the crucial election of 1977, nearly one-third of the Muslim votes went to the opponents of Congress.

Since it was the six groups we have described – namely, the Brahmins, Banias, Patidars, Kshatriyas, Christians and Muslims – who played an important part in the politics of Anand, we shall confine our analysis to these ethnic groups only.

THE INSTITUTIONS OF ANAND

Among the institutions of Anand, the most important ones to note are the civic, educational and economic ones. We shall consider some of these in detail.

(a) The municipality
Anand Municipality, as stated earlier, came into existence in 1884. In the initial period its membership was divided into official and non-official categories and members were elected to the latter on a limited franchise. Subsequently, such a classification and limits on franchise were dropped.

In Anand ambitious men, with or without the backing of the Congress Party, contested elections. The Congress Party was reluctant to lend its name openly to its members but it often connived at their claim that the organisation was behind them. The absence of party organisations within the civic body often led to shifting coalitions, instability and supersession of the elected body. Whenever the municipality was superseded, it was administered by a nominee of the state government. A significant change occurred in the late 1960s when the Swatantra Party, after a good showing in the elections of 1962 and 1967, decided to contest seats in the civic body *as* a political party.

Among the contestants for election there were Patidars, mostly employed in the grain trade, and some Kshatriyas. Very few came forward from other ethnic groups.

Throughout the struggle for Indian independence the import- ance of the civic body as a school for democracy was emphasised. It was very much hoped that after independence the civic body would help solve the growing problem of services in urban India, and that it would also attract talented and dedicated men who would then put their mind to its solution.

But what the people of Anand witnessed was something different. From the election of members down to the implementation of policies, the civic body failed to live up to the expectations of its citizens. The city fathers often took unfair advantage of their position. So very poor did the reputation of civic bodies become that men of integrity were deterred from attempting to gain office.

In 1967, with the entry of the Swatantra Party into the civic body, its performance began to improve. The party put forward a panel of candidates and a specific programme and won the election. Its youthful group of councillors, often dubbed as *Juvanias* (young and inexperienced), redeemed most of their electoral pledges. They provided extended facilities for drinking water, drainage and electricity. They widened roads and built markets. In a short time Anand received a tremendous facelift. But when it came to town planning, they too got bogged down, for they dared not go against their own supporters.

During the emergency a pro-Congress group emerged and the bi-partisan character of the civic body improved its tone.

(b) Educational institutions

One of the major institutions of Anand, and one which exercised great influence on the region, is the Charotar Education Society (CES). Started by a group of dedicated volunteers, the CES was responsible for bringing about enormous changes in the educational and, through it, in the economic life of Anand. It also succeeded in protecting itself from ambitious individuals who often treated educational institutions as a power base for their wider interest in politics.

Right from the start, in 1916 the CES adopted a different kind of approach to education. Its founder, Motibhai Amin, was deeply influenced by the model of the Deccan Education Society in Poona, where highly dedicated teachers acted as volunteers, offered their services at a nominal salary and the institutions looked after the residential, medical and educational needs of their children. The CES of Anand was modelled on the same lines. The moral authority of such dedicated men proved to be a great asset when dealing with the educational bureaucracy at the time of the British. It also helped the CES to collect donations in the district, in the rest of the country, and in East Africa, where the Patidars from the region had flourished in trade and commerce. Finally, it gained the CES the abiding loyalty of its own students, a number of whom rose to high position, in Gujarat and outside.

The CES ran a number of educational institutions. There great emphasis was put on the need to be receptive to Western ideas of science and technology without sacrificing the indigenous religions and cultural traditions. It also underlined the need for voluntary social work, together with the importance of public participation. One of its foremost schools was named after the well-known nationalist leader, Dadabhai Navroji (DN). The DN High School produced men who made a mark not only in business, industry and the professions, but also in politics. In fact most of the political elite in the district were the product of the DN High School.

Educational institutions proliferated in Anand. Agriculturists, industrialists, the professional classes and those resident in East Africa preferred to send their children to Anand to be educated, recognising the quality of the education their children would receive. At the same time they were also assured of the fact that their children would not be uprooted from their cultural background. By 1971/72 nearly one-third of Anand's population consisted of students.

Anand and its vicinity also became a centre for higher and technical education. In order to provide facilities for higher education to the students in the district, the Sardar Patel University came into existence in 1955. Prior to its establishment students went either to Baroda or Ahmedabad, with little or no assurance that they would be admitted to the much sought-after faculties of science, technology and agriculture. The new university did extremely well in the field of technology. Its products stimulated the growth of small- and medium-scale industrial units in the district.

Earlier, in 1937, the Institute of Agriculture was established in order to stimulate agricultural developments in the region and to improve a special breed of cows. The institute received a tremendous boost with the coming of independence. It now provides training and research facilities in animal husbandry, dairying, agronomy, plant breeding, pathology and bacteriology, entomology, agricultural chemistry, soil science and veterinary services. The agricultural prosperity of the region owes a great deal to this institute.

The moving force behind the university as well as the institute

were men who were tired of being pushed around by arrogant
members of the Congress Party and were therefore actively engaged
in building a viable opposition to it. The founder of the university
was Bhailalbhai Patel and that of the institute, K. M. Munshi. Both
of them were actively involved in building up the Swatantra Party.
Consequently the university and the institute have both had a
troubled beginning at the hands of the ruling Congress Party.

(c) Economic institutions
One of the largest milk co-operatives of the world, popularly known
as AMUL, is located in Anand. It has not only brought prosperity to
Anand and its district but has also stimulated the growth of similar
milk dairies, based on the principle of co-operatives, in other parts of
India. It is considered to be one of the largest industrial units in this
rapidly industrialising region. It also represents one of the rare
instances where politicians have worked in close co-operation with a
highly dedicated techno-managerial class drawn from practically
all parts of India.

AMUL grew up as an offshoot of the Indian national movement
with the sole purpose of protecting the farmers of the district from
the ruthless milk contractors of the Second World War. They fixed
its price and made huge profits for themselves. Sardar Patel advised
the farmers to launch a *satyagraha* against the monopolistic restrictions imposed on them by the then Bombay government. The
authorities gave in, and in December 1946 the Kaira District Co-
operative Milk Producers' Union (AMUL) came into existence.

Farmers, politicians and the techno-managerial class have all
played an important part in forming the co-operative. The two
principal architects of AMUL were Tribhuvandas Patel (T. K.)
and V. Kurien, a technical manager with a great gift for building up
and running complex organisations. T. K. and Kurien not only
ideally complemented each other, but also succeeded in keeping the
organisation of AMUL and its vast resources out of party politics.

The milk co-operative units of Amul have now spread to all the
villages of the district. And they are run on democratic lines. Unlike
village *panchayats* (councils), they are run in the most businesslike
fashion with minimum disruption. Since a part of people's livelihood depends on them, both managerial efficiency and participation are very much prized. In a sense these milk co-operative
units have been the most effective means of involving the rural
population in the democratic process itself.[26]

Besides AMUL, the two other major economic complexes of Anand and its vicinity are the Sardargunj grain market and the industrial corporation of Vithal Udyognagar on the outskirts of the town.

2 Social Cohesion and the Decline of Political Homogeneity[1]

In his theory of social status, Max Weber made an incisive distinction between caste and status based on ethnicity:

> A 'status' segregation grown into a 'caste' differs in its structure from a mere ethnic segregation: the caste structure transforms the horizontal and unconnected coexistences of ethnically segregated groups into a vertical social system of super and subordination.[2]

In other words, in an ethnic structure, differences among groups run on horizontal and parallel lines, whereas in a caste structure, due to the peculiar historical reasons, such differences become vertical and hierarchical.[3] Moreover, in societies with parallel co-existence, ethnic communities are allowed to consider their honour as the higher one, whereas in those with hierarchical stratification, honour declines as you go down the vertical structure.[4] The valid question to ask in this connection is whether or not, with the help of an egalitarian political ideology, the 'transformation' of a horizontal differentiation into a vertical one can be reversed, segmentally, in terms of political status and participation.

But before we examine this question in detail we must note that the consequences of interaction between a political system based on egalitarian norms, and a vertically differentiated social organisation based on the principles of hierarchy, will be materially different from those of a social organisation which is only horizontally differentiated. This is because in a horizontal arrangement some measure of social equality between different ethnic groups is already in existence. And as far as the caste-ridden society with vertical social organisation is concerned the egalitarian norms of the democratic political system will create conditions for equality in the political field to begin with.

At least in the *political* field, therefore, the new political system is likely to fill in the differentia which came about as a result of the peculiar evolution of the vertical system. In actual effect the new political system will impose a new structure of formal political relations from *outside*, enfranchising everyone regardless of his or her position in the social hierarchy. It will also provide institutional facilities for questioning and rejecting many status-oriented privileges. This will allow some scope for circumventing the disadvantages in the political field which were imposed by a vertically differentiated society.[5] Thus, in its interaction with the democratic political system the vertical society acquires an added character: while it remains, socially hierarchical in the initial period, it moves, in a politico-legal sense, closer to the horizontally differentiated society with a momentum for further political change.

The egalitarian norms, which split apart each group from its vertical ties in politics, also put into motion processes of differentiation *within* such groups. Such a continuing momentum of change, not inhibited by the problems of ethnicity in democratic politics, is likely to go a long way.

The problem of ethnicity in the democratic politics of Western countries provides an interesting background. A lively controversy exists in the literature on the persistence of ethnicity in voting in Western democracies, in particular in the USA. Robert Dahl, in his seminal work *Who Governs?*, found that in New Haven politics, '. . . in spite of growing assimilation, ethnic factors continued to make themselves felt with astonishing tenacity',[6] and expressed the hope that in the second and the third generation voting the importance of national origin 'surely must recede'.

His co-researcher, Raymond Wolfinger, disagreed. According to Wolfinger, social mobility, and more specifically the emergence of a middle class in the ethnic group, *reinforced* ethnicity in politics. In his view,

> Ethnic voting will be greatest when the ethnic group has produced a middle class, i.e., in the second and third generations, not in the first. Furthermore, the shifts in party identification resulting from this first major candidacy will persist beyond the election in which they occurred.[7]

Michael Parenti, who took issue with Dahl, argued that at the root of the problem was the latter's inability to make a distinction between what Parsons called 'acculturation' and 'assimilation'.[8] By adopting the life-style, language, norms and various social practices of the host society, the ethnic groups become acculturated rather than assimilated into it. Nevertheless, such processes allow them to continue as ethnic blocks for voting and other purposes, if they so choose.

A much more definitive judgement on the persistence of the ethnic character of American society was put forward in the celebrated volume *Beyond the Melting Pot* by Nathan Glazer and Daniel Moynihan. The authors bluntly stated their position in their opening lines as follows: 'The point about the melting pot . . . is that it did not happen.'[9] Furthermore, according to the authors, the ethnic mosaic persisted as the basic factor in the social and political life of the USA.

In the pages that follow I shall examine in detail the relationship between the vertically differentiated social organisation and the democratic political system in India. The structural change in the political system, from colonial to democratic, with its implicit norms, has succeeded in inducing differentiated electoral choices even within a social organisation which in its primary social concerns still discourages equality and diversity. Various explanations have been suggested to describe the relationship between caste and democratic politics on the one hand, and the agents of democratic socialisation on the other. I shall now examine each of them in some detail.

The relationship between caste and democratic institutions in India has been the main focus of attention of students of Indian studies for nearly a quarter of a century. It has presented a many-sided challenge to social analysts as a problem in structural-functionalism, social interaction and political dynamism. Invariably, in this relationship, the political element is thought to be growing progressively stronger and at times catalysing other forces. As a result, it has inspired a lot of lively writing on the theme of social change. At the theoretical level a number of ideas have been put forward to explain the interaction between the traditional social organisation based on the principle of hierarchy and the new political institutions inspired by the norms of equality. Some of the explanations have been motivated by the search for an all-explanatory theory of the Indian socio-political system, based on an all-pervading single factor somewhat similar to the Marxian theory of class, the analogue in the Indian contexts being caste. Other explanations go in search of adaptive structures, which according to Parsons help societies out of their discordant situations. Adaptive structures in the Indian context are supposed to take the form of caste associations, which supposedly lessen the traumatic shock of political modernisation by smoothly forging the operative relationship between the traditional society and the new political institutions. The single-factor explanations treat caste as a cohesive unit even in politics, whereas the explanations based on adaptive structure, because of the inevitable power rivalries and cleavages within caste association, identify increasing political differentiation within the voluntary body. The theories of caste association also treat it as a vital means of political socialisation.

I shall argue, however, that both these sets of explanations are simplistic and ambiguous, that they tend to treat caste in politics abstractly rather than to examine the actual involvement of specific castes in their day-to-day politics in empirically testable situations over an extended period of time. The bulk of castes in India do not have caste associations: what they have instead are caste councils (caste panchayats) which merely address themselves to the primary social concerns of the caste – namely, endogamy, ritual and pollution. A distinction, therefore, has to be made between those castes which add voluntary structures, such as caste associations, to their existing ascriptive body and those which do not. Here again, one must empirically determine the answer to the crucial question: To what extent is the primary social cohesion of the ascriptive structure available to such newly added voluntary bodies? Finally, one needs to take a hard look at the function of political socialisation attributed to caste associations wherever they exist. In my view these associations do not always perform such a function. At times they even seek to set back the political clock. Indeed, the present research suggests that fragments of castes, dispersed in different areas, get inducted into the political system and receive far more effective grass-roots political socialisation than they do through the efforts of caste association.

I shall substantiate these and other assertions with the help of the material collected in the field-work in Gujarat, which extended for seven years in a rural community and for ten years in an urban community. It will be the argument of this chapter that in order to explain the interaction between castes and democratic institutions in India we need a theory of cohesion which can identify the extent of caste solidarity when it is engaged in three different kinds of pursuit: (a) in preserving itself as an endogamous unit with a distinct social identity within the Hindu social organisation; (b) in seeking a predetermined social mobility and pressing for higher social recognition; and (c) in searching for better economic opportunities or a share in political power or both. The extent of cohesion that castes can muster when engaged in these three different pursuits is not always the same.

This chapter, then, will focus on the following main topics: the Srinivas-Harrison model of the subsumption of the new political institutions into the caste system; the Weiner-Rudolphs model of caste association and the consequent increasing political differentiation within castes, and my own model of levels of caste cohesion, leadership bifurcation and decision-making fragmentation; it will also discuss political stimulus and response in a rural community, the social cohesion and political differences that exist in an urban community, and the emerging horizontal fragmentation of decision-making units.

I THE SRINIVAS-HARRISON MODEL

The cultural anthropologist M. N. Srinivas, a prolific and perceptive writer on caste, has expressed the view that the establishment of the Pax Britannica provided the various castes on India with the opportunity of overcoming the 'severe limits on the horizontal extension of . . . ties'[10] which were imposed on them by the pre-British fragmentary political kingdoms in India. Added to this the increased facilities for communication and transport brought together men of the same castes who were 'scattered in far-flung villages'.[11] Long before parliamentary institutions were established in India, the networks of social organisation on caste lines had proliferated. Such networks in the post-independence period were used in order to influence votes, which in turn evoked 'widespread condemnation of exploitation of caste-links for election purposes'[12] from the national leaders. Because the social organisation of the castes on horizontal lines had preceded the introduction of democratic ideology, they found it easier to subsume the new political institutions.

This thesis of Srinivas was much more effectively articulated by Selig Harrison in his case-study of caste in Andhra politics, which mainly concentrated on the politics of the castes in the Andhra state legislature. Pushing Srinivas's thesis to its logical conclusion, Harrison argued his case from a model of caste-party identity, according to which the two peasant castes of Andhra, the Kammas and Reddis, first united to dislodge the Brahmins from power, then fell apart as a result of political rivalry and joined two different political parties. The Kammas joined the Communist Party and the Reddis the Congress Party.[13] In Harrison's view, therefore, the nature of political cleavage in Andhra was none other than the politically transformed social cleavage between the two peasant castes.

Harrison's work, despite its pessimism and its failure to provide a helpful model, was one of the finest contributions to Indian political sociology, unsurpassed to this date, in my view. So persuasive was his argument that a generation of students of Indian studies did not even get down to questioning his model of caste-party identity against the background of the electoral data that he had provided – data that, in fact, did not fully substantiate his thesis.[14]

II   THE WEINER-RUDOLPHS MODEL

From the point of view of the impact of the new political ideology on the traditional social organisation of the castes, its induction into the political system and the consequences of this, some of the most sophisticated arguments are those of Myron Weiner and the Rudolphs. Their writings brought a host of structural-functional perspectives and explanations into the field of Indian studies. The Rudolphs actually concluded from their functionalist analysis, that Indians had a genius for adaptation and assimilation when faced with the possibility of conflict and disruption.

Weiner rejected the traditional-modern dichotomy on the grounds that it regarded traditionalism as 'temporary and reactionary' and modernity as 'the wave of the future'.[15] In reality, 'as economic growth has occurred in India and political awareness has increased, the number of community associations has grown'. Further, 'within political parties ascriptive identifications are playing a prominent role' and the major social institutions, with the exception of family and kinship units, 'have associations that articulate their interests'. While each of these institutions may not have its own political associations, 'increasingly, such groupings have had their political manifestations'.[16]

It is indeed impossible to say that each caste in India – and there are more than 3000 of them[17] – has an association which articulates its interests. What most of them probably do is merely seek out whatever guarantees the survival of their cultural identity within the Hindu social organisation. It would also be true to say that the great majority do not aspire to play a political role as castes. What one comes across, time and time again, in the field-work is that political parties and electioneering candidates in search of support explore the possibility of using the social cohesion and communication channels of various castes. In that fashion, fragments of certain castes get inducted into the political process, while others do not. What portions of localised fragments of a caste get mobilised by parties and their candidates can be empirically determined. It would be misleading therefore, to suggest that the whole caste as a caste gets politically mobilised and comes out with 'political manifestations'. In my view, empirical confirmation of the extent of political mobilisation of certain castes such as the Kshatriyas, Nadars and Jats, which did get massively involved in political activity, will dispel the *en bloc* view of caste politicisation.

Weiner made a questionable inference that, given the conditions of economic development and growth of political consciousness, castes in India came to acquire economic interests and political ambition of their own as castes and to give themselves voluntary associations to be able to pursue them. Nevertheless, he did raise a few pertinent questions: What in fact does happen to the primary social cohesion of a caste when it is confronted with a new set of problems? Does it always take on non-social and non-traditional functions as a caste? To what extent is it able to retain its primary social cohesion when it takes on new roles and functions? These and other related questions will be examined in the next section.

Lloyd and Susanne Rudolph made a fascinating attempt at developing what they called 'the sociology of caste associations'. They started where Weiner had left off. While Weiner was engaged in identifying the emergence of caste association and its roles and functions, the Rudolphs in *The Modernity of Tradition* took for granted its existence in all parts of India.[18] The question they asked was: In what way do the norms of a voluntary body such as the caste association exercise influence on the caste itself? They contended that the influence of such norms and of the institutional facilities on the caste was enormous. In their words,

Caste is losing the functions, norms and structure once associated with it and acquiring new ones. It is serving the ritual and occupational goals of traditional society less, the mobility and participation goals of modern society more. In doing so, it [the ascriptive-voluntary body] helps to substitute in the lives of ordinary Indians choice for birth, equality for hierarchy, and opportunity for fate.[19]

Once a voluntary body was added on to the caste, they argued, the norms of the former began to prevail upon those of the latter. The Rudolphs, as a matter of fact, saw the 'reincarnation'[20] of caste in caste associations, and for all practical purposes they treated the associations as agents of change. By means of caste associations, they argued, the teeming millions of India, born in the rigid ascriptive structures of castes, were being homogenised, secularised, and democratised into the new ways of democratic society.[21] What made such a transformation smoother was 'corporatism' all the way: from the corporation of caste to the modern corporatism of the caste association with little or no intervening 'individualist' phase as in the case of Western countries.[22]

The Rudolphs provided a sophisticated model of the political mobilisation capacity of caste associations. The model helped them to identify three different types of mobilisation: vertical, horizontal and differential, depending upon the stage of development and internal integration of particular castes.[23] The vertical mobilisation took place through the effort of 'traditional notables'; horizontal mobilisation by means of integration of caste fragments spread over dispersed areas; and differentiated mobilisation through the efforts of political parties, differently appealing to different segments of caste in terms of 'ideology, sentiment and interest'.[24]

Once an ascriptive body such as the caste 'reincarnates' itself into a voluntary caste association, internal differences and cleavages within the caste come to acquire a political significance. Political parties further help articulate their differences. 'It is in this sense,' the Rudolphs argued, 'that modern politics appears to be an instrument for both the revival and the supersession of traditional society'.[25]

The Rudolphs' model rests on the assumption that caste means the same thing to all people belonging to Hindu social organisation. While they start off with the view that different castes possess different degrees of internal cohesion, their picture of the caste is largely deduced from a model of the rising peasant castes or groups of castes such as the Kshatriyas, the Nadars, the Jats, etc. These castes have certain common characteristics but it would be misleading to say that all other castes share them. Since some castes have caste associations the Rudolphs wrongly assume that all other castes also have them. Not all the castes in India have caste associations in the sense of voluntary organisations looking after economic and political problems. The bulk of them have caste councils, and they are integrally connected with the maintenance of the ascriptive character of castes.

Further, the Rudolphs have attributed the functions of homogenisation, secularisation and democratisation to caste associations,[26] using sweeping generalisations about the activities of caste associations to support their assertion. This point being most crucial, specific empirical support in favour of their argument would have been most helpful. On the other hand, as we shall presently see, the fragments of castes attained a fair measure of political socialisation and internalisation of the norms of the new political institutions despite the self-seeking activities of some of the office-bearers of caste associations. Some of the leaders of the caste associations, such as the Kshatriya Sabha, wanted to desecularise whatever electoral differentiation and secularity had been attained through day-to-day political involvement by the Kshatriyas in a rural community in Gujarat. Finally, the Kshatriya Sabha as a caste association did not aim at the homogenisation of the group of castes which called themselves Kshatriyas, nor did its activities have that result. On the contrary its domination by the princely order resulted in a revolt led by a leadership of humbler origin – a revolt which on the eve of the General Election of 1967 finally split the organisation into two groups: the Kshatriya Sabha and the Kshatriya Seva Samaj. In conclusion, then, one must recognise that in the process of homogenisation, secularisation, and democratisation which is evident in rural as well as urban India, factors such as increased emphasis on education, accelerated pace of industrialisation, better facilities for transport and communication, the growth of regional language presses, the growing awareness of economic and administrative problems, intensely contested elections, and, above all, political involvement in local situations, all merit due recognition. These processes were not set in motion by caste associations, and the influence on political participation exerted on members of castes by existing associations requires specific and rigorous analysis. Broad theoretical formulations in these areas initially help us to identify problem situations; by themselves they do not make our knowledge certain. Certain knowledge requires the rigorous empirical test of hypotheses deduced from the theory.

III   A MODEL FOR SOCIAL COHESION, LEADERSHIP AND DECISION-MAKING

The initial consumers of all scientific knowledge are the practitioners of the science itself: they check and test its explicit assertions and underlying assumptions. Such an exercise, however, cannot be undertaken if the theoretical formulations are couched in blanket terms. So far as the phenomenon of caste and democratic institutions is concerned, the blanket terms 'caste association',[27] 'caste federation',[28] 'adaptive structure'[29] are used in order to explain the entire range of operative relationships between the caste as a unit of traditional society and the superimposed modern democratic institutions and procedures. These at best explain one or two specific aspects of their relationships.

Difficulties arise when caste in politics is taken to mean the participation by a caste with its social cohesion and communication network intact. The problem is further complicated when voluntary dimensions of 'association' and complex co-operative dimensions of 'federation' are added on to a strictly ascriptive structure such as a caste. Taken at their dictionary meanings 'caste' and 'association' are as much opposites as are 'ascriptive' and 'voluntary'. The use of the term 'caste association' can only indicate an association of some people of the same caste but not of the entire caste. In making such a distinction what is underlined is that the extent of cohesion and the communication network available to a caste for its primary social concerns, which makes it an ascriptive body, cannot be taken for granted when only some members of it band themselves into an 'association' and seek to pursue non-traditional goals.

Among others, the concerns of a caste are the primary social ones of endogamy, ritual and pollution, as has already been said. In the realisation of those goals a caste enjoys maximum internal cohesion and the most effective use of its communication network. Such traditional concerns are basic to the caste's survival as an ascriptive structure with a distinct cultural identity of its own within the Hindu social organisation; when a caste moves from these concerns towards a search for higher social recognition, greater economic opportunities and a share in political power, its internal cohesion becomes progressively weaker. The search for social recognition, which is an attempt in the direction of ascriptive regeneration and a more desired position within the social hierarchy, may be blessed, sectionally or wholly, with the same extent of cohesion and sense of togetherness as exists in a caste when it pursues its primary social concerns. But a caste's economic and political drives necessarily lead it to an internal competition for enhanced status, material gain, and, therefore, to dissensions in the pursuit of specific goals and rivalry for power positions in general. It is therefore pointless to talk about the presence of the same extent of cohesion in a caste for its economic and political pursuits as exists for its social pursuits. A caste engaged in the former is not even caste-like in its concerns, which traditionally speaking are primarily social, and therefore anything other than that becomes the concern not of the caste but of a group of members acting on its behalf. As opposed to the maximum cohesion arising out of the basic social concerns of a caste, its economic and political pursuits involve appeals to new identity, economic gain, power and status, each of which is a potential divider. Hence, each of the new appeals is invariably prefaced with a call for unity.

In order to grasp the operative relationship between castes and the newly established democratic institutions in India we therefore require a model which can address itself to the following: differentiation in the internal cohesion of the caste; differentiation in its leadership; and horizontal or factional segmentation of its decision-making units. Let us examine each of these in some detail.

PRIMARY, SECONDARY AND TERTIARY LEVELS OF CASTE COHESION

It is important to note here that the quality and extent of cohesion of a caste changes from one kind of pursuit to another. A caste enjoys the explicit or tacit concurrence and support of all its members when it is engaged in those functions which maintain its distinct cultural identity. It maintains this by its firm grip both on endogamy and, to a lesser extent, on matters relating to ritual and to pollution. It treats these three functions as its *raison d'être* and demands the support of the entire group towards their realisation. Pursuit of these and the maintenance of the norms implicit in them equally become the concern of all, although the caste leaders, mostly venerated old men, became formally responsible for overall supervision through the caste councils.

When a caste strives for higher social recognition within the Hindu social organisation, it takes up on itself a new non-traditional function. For such a purpose a caste has to demonstrate a higher ritual standard, which becomes a responsibility of all its members.[30] To achieve such a goal the caste elders require the assistance of a new set of leaders to help them formulate a rationale for the drive, carry on public relations work, enter into complex and often tough negotiations with the leaders of other castes and administrators, formulate strategies and execute tactics.[31] While the traditional and non-traditional leaders together launch such a drive, the outcome of their efforts affects all the members of the caste.[32]

Such a venture on the part of the caste is able to induce a secondary cohesion because while all the members are affected by such a drive forward, and even have to conform to ritual norms higher than those they were used to, the bulk of its members remain passive participants. Their participation in such a venture obviously is not of the same quality, intensity and scope as in the case of the basic social concerns of the caste – namely, endogamy, ritual, and pollution. As a matter of fact in the caste's drive towards higher social recognition, its internal cohesion is stretched to its optimum limits. Such a cohesion, then, is secondary, because it is not a part of deeply ingrained traditional behaviour directed towards achieving the age-old social goals, but is something that is rationally put across, with a sharper role-distinction between the leaders and the followers, and directed towards a social destiny which is new and unfamiliar.

Finally, there is the tertiary level of cohesion. When a caste is engaged in the drive to secure better economic opportunities or a share in political power or the appointment of a caste member to public office, not everyone in the caste is either involved or directly affected. In gossip groups among the rank and file one often hears a sharp distinction drawn between those who would directly benefit by such a drive and the rest. The leaders, likely to benefit by such a drive, exhort their followers to support them. Since such drives are thus out-and-out non-traditional ones, lacking in religious sanction and in social organisational reference, they display a tertiary level of cohesion of the caste or factions within it. From start to finish such drives are considered suspect, in that they are in the interest of the few, and therefore politically divisive. Castes which get involved in such drives progressively lose whatever cohesion they are able to muster at the tertiary level without lessening their cohesion at the primary social level. Even in a politically divided caste, the basic social function of supervising endogamy, ritual and pollution remains unaffected. Table 2.1 summarises the relationships within the caste and the levels of cohesion.

TABLE 2.1. Caste and three levels of cohesion

Extent of cohesion	*Extent of involvement of its members*	*Nature of cohesion*
(1) Maintaining a distinct cultural identity within the Hindu social organisation by means of its basic social concerns: endogamy, ritual, and pollution.	All members of caste equally affected and equally involved. Formal role-distinction between the caste veterans and the rest.	Traditional goals pursued through deeply ingrained behaviour. Feeling of oneness on the part of the whole caste. Primary cohesion brought about by means of ascriptive togetherness.
(2) Seeking greater social recognition; emulation of higher ritual standards.	All members of caste equally affected but not equally involved. Some become effective leaders. Role-distinction between leaders and followers clearly recognised.	Non-traditional goals rationally conceived and widely shared. Deliberately brought about group support and unity. Secondary cohesion.
(3) Seeking better economic opportunities and greater share in political power.	Few affected and fewer actively involved. The rest become onlookers, suspicious or hostile. Voiced or unvoiced distinction between those who would benefit and the rest.	Material goals and plea for identification with the cause. Mystique of group importance and benefit. Uncertain group support and potential divisions. Tertiary cohesion.

BIFURCATION OF SOCIAL AND POLITICAL LEADERSHIP IN CASTES AT THE GRASS-ROOTS LEVEL

The operation of grass-roots democratic institutions, now nearly a quarter of a century old, has brought about a significant shift towards leadership differentiation within the castes. The venerated old leaders, who sat on the caste councils as well as the statutory panchayats, have by and large withdrawn themselves from the panchayats. Relatively younger men have taken charge of the statutory bodies. The reasons for such a differentiation are manifold: new norms and new mechanisms of decision-making introduced by democratic political institutions which remain inconsistent with the traditional ways of arriving at decisions; the decline of respect for age and in some cases familial status; the questioning political culture introduced by democracy; and, above all, the needed skill in coalition-building across castes for which the elders had neither experience nor aptitude.

The net effect of such a leadership differentiation on the general cohesion of the caste is worth noting. Traditional respectability remained with the social leaders and they continued to enjoy caste-wide support in social matters. Political leadership, on the other hand, came to be associated with the seamy side of politics where people with money, leisure, manipulative dispositions, devious methods, etc., seemed to be caught up in frictions and engaged in power games and the pursuit of personal glory. Consequently, the support received by the political leaders was for the caste *per se* rather than for what they did or stood for. Since politics did not and could not become one of the primary concerns of the caste, faction-building and divisiveness could easily develop. What has finally emerged out of the bifurcation of leadership is an insulated social cohesion on the one hand, and an ever increasing political differentiation on the other.

FRAGMENTATION OF THE DECISION-MAKING UNITS OF THE CASTE

The decisions about the primary social concerns of the caste are made by the caste council and affect all the persons belonging to the caste; it is difficult, however, to find any similarly binding decision-making machinery for the non-social matters of the caste. Once we move away from the basic social concerns of the caste what we notice is the fragmentation in its decision-making processes on horizontal and factional lines. Because of the attenuation of caste cohesion in non-social matters, and also because of the separation of its social and political leadership, the effective area of decision-making often shrinks from the caste as a whole to its sub-units; i.e. those of family, extended family, kin-group neighbourhood, kin-group spread over several villages, and endogamous units within the caste.

Of these, the most effective unit of social interaction and decision-making on a large range of issues, including the political, is the kin-group neighbourhood and factions within it, or those that cut across such neighbourhoods. Within them, where to vote is decided in the same fashion as which school to send one's children to, which doctor or lawyer to consult, where to go shopping, which film to go to, etc. – collectively and with one's circle of acquaintances. On all such issues group decision-making in the neighbourhood is a way of life in which decisions on political matters are no exception. In a multi-kin-group or a multi-caste neighbourhood, the framework of decision-making would correspond to the framework of social interaction.

In such socially interactive decision-making groups, influential individuals play an important part. Such neighbourhood fragments are often linked through the liaison of influential persons by political parties and electioneering candidates. To be effective in a caste or multi-caste neighbourhood a candidate must have those with influence on his side. The flow of political influence is directed essentially through them. In that sense the framework of electoral influence is no different from the one described in *The People's Choice*, especially in the theory of the two-step flow of communication, which holds that the media influence 'the opinion leaders' first, and they in turn influence 'the less active sections of the population'.[33] The present analysis substitutes the electioneering candidate or his agents for the media, wherever the media are not a significant factor.

What is thought of as the 'caste vote' or caste 'vote bank'[34] is essentially a successful piecing together of horizontally, geographically and fractionally segmented votes scattered over different neighbourhood groupings of the same caste. Even in such instances, neighbourhood electoral diversity is as much of a possibility as homogeneity.

In the following section I shall illustrate, with the help of my field data, the significance of the bifurcation of social and political leadership for the political development of a rural community, especially for the growth within the community of a dynamic cross-caste political cleavage structure.[35] The section after that will illustrate the proliferating political differentiation, despite social cohesion, in an urban community. In both these cases the part played by the only politically active caste association, the Kshatriya Sabha, was marginal.

IV POLITICAL STIMULUS AND RESPONSE IN A RURAL COMMUNITY

A continuing field-study of a village near Baroda conducted intensively during four periods between 1959 and 1971 did not confirm the view that the castes get inducted into the democratic process by means of 'caste associations'. Out of the four politically significant castes – Patidars (8 per cent), Kshatriyas (46 per cent), Vasavas (14 per cent), and Venkars (ex-untouchables, 7 per cent) – only the Kshatriyas were approached by their so-called caste association, the Kshatriya Sabha, during the General Elections of 1962, 1967 and 1971. On each occasion the bulk of Kshatriyas did not heed its electoral instructions and, indeed, branded the body as an organisation of the upper-crust Rajputs interested in mobilising political support on behalf of vested interests and feudal elements. The Kshatriyas of the village were politically socialised into the ways of democratic politics like any other caste in the village: by means of actual political participation.

The village had undergone a major political change – from non-elected to elected political institutions – without the help of caste associations, political parties or brokers. When the democratic institutions were introduced in the village, various castes, at different levels of political development and internal cohesion, responded differently to the structural changes. Subsequently as a result of their operational involvement and by emulating one another, they learned a great deal about the new political system.

The two peasant castes, the Patidars (landowning and politically dominant) and the Kshatriyas (numerically powerful) became continually involved in a struggle for power and office in the village. Through their strategies and counter-strategies they stimulated each other into becoming more politically flexible and skilful in building a multi-caste base of political power. The Vasavas and the Venkars, too, learned through social and political emulation, and began to play their role as auxiliary social group more effectively. In the last analysis the twin teachers of democracy for these four castes were the gradual internalisation of the norms of the new ideology on the one hand, and actual political involvement on the other.[36]

At the root of the political change in the village was the bifurcation of its social and political leadership, a necessary and sufficient condition of increasing political differentiation in otherwise socially cohesive castes. For after the major structural change in the mid-1950s, which required the local council to be constituted on the basis of universal adult suffrage, the rough-and-tumble of democratic politics pushed into the background the old and venerated leaders of the Patidars as well as the Kshatriyas. Until then these men had retained the dual role of social and political leadership. Since 1904, when the statutory local council was established in the village, the Patidar elders, belonging to the families with high status in the caste, had sat on the statutory body as well as on their caste council. The same was true of the Kshatriya elders whenever they got themselves nominated to the statutory council along with the Patidars.

Among the Patidars one of the earliest repercussions of the introduction of universal adult suffrage was an excessive questioning and criticism by their own younger men of their ability and role as members of the council. A similar barrage of criticism was directed towards the elder Kshatriya membership by its own younger men. For a long time the Kshatriya elders had accepted a position that was subordinate to the Patidars. That was clearly unacceptable to the politically ambitious, articulate and restless younger Kshatriyas.

The Patidar elders faded away from the political scene without incident. The Kshatriya elders did not. The impatience of their younger men brought into play kinship differences among their two major groups. It therefore took a little longer for the Kshatriya elders to hand over power to their younger men.

The emulative framework of village politics also helped the Venkars to bifurcate their leadership along the lines of the Patidars and the Kshatriyas. Until 1971, the wave of bifurcation had not affected the Vasavas: this was because their involvement in village politics, until recently, was only marginal.

The Patidars, as well as Kshatriya elders, however, relinquished merely the political leadership of their respective groups; they continued to be in command of the social leadership of their castes. Political leadership of the two castes was taken on by the younger men initially from the families which had also provided social leadership. Thus for a short period the familial status had continued to be the basis of the differentiated social and political leadership. It took another wave of change in these two castes to undermine the importance of certain families, and this happened more than a decade after the introduction of democracy, when familial status in the political realm also was challenged by still younger men in these two contending castes. The decline of familial status was marked by a corresponding rise in the importance of political skill in building inter-caste, inter-clan and at times even more diversified bases of political power. Henceforth the politically ambitious neither confined themselves to their own caste nor took for granted its support. Political support became for them a matter of skilful accomodation, manipulation and contrivance. So far as local politics went, such skills had to be put to work within a highly structured situation of castes and regard for personalities. National electoral politics on the other hand, provided the politically ambitious with much greater freedom and scope for cross-caste political cleavages. Some of these cross-cutting political cleavages in national politics inevitably affected the style and character of local politics.[37] Differentiated political leadership thus became an agent of political diversification within the castes in local as well as national politics.

In their contest for seats in the village council Patidars opposed Patidars with support from the Kshatriyas and vice-versa. The support of the rest of the castes in the village for these two contending groups became increasingly differentiated. But much greater diversity of support than in the elections of the village council was evident inside the council for the election of its chairmen and other positions. The Patidars and the Kshatriyas alternately got themselves elected to the chairmanship of the council by manipulating the cleavages in each other's ranks.

The process of diversification of political support across castes was accentuated by the General Elections of 1962, 1967 and 1971. Each time, because of the presentation of issues and the political pulls during campaigns, the cleavage structure of village politics changed. Instead of conforming to the existing political divisions in the village, the new cleavage structure preceding General Elections cut across such divisions.

V SOCIAL COHESION AND POLITICAL DIFFERENCES IN AN URBAN COMMUNITY

My intensive field-work in Anand revealed an increasing political differentiation in castes whose primary social cohesion remained more or less unchanged. The data confirm the view that the primarily social cohesion of a caste is not easily transferable to its non-social pursuits. Political homogeneity was never attained by most castes, including the Kshatriyas, even though Anand is one of the more vigorous centres of the caste association of the Kshatriyas (the Kshatriya Sabha) and the home of one of its splinter groups, the Kshatriya Seva Samaj. Whenever political homogeneity was achieved by a caste, my field data indicate, it was not because of its 'caste association', assuming there was one. Indeed, by and large, the cohesiveness of the caste in non-social matters did not go beyond primary groups such as the extended family or kinship neighbourhood. This contention is substantiated in findings on the six major social and religious groups of Anand which together comprise nearly three-quarters of Anand's population. They are the Brahmins (7 per cent), Banias (5 per cent), Patidars (22 per cent), Kshatriyas (25 per cent), Christians (4 per cent) and Muslims (8 per cent). The two religious minorities, Christians and Muslims, are included to permit comparison of changes in political homogeneity among them as well.

In order to grasp the political background of the respondents, an attempt was made to ascertain the tradition of their family vote, a fairly reliable index of a voter's political background. The response was as set out in Table 2.2.

TABLE 2.2. The General Election of 1952: caste and voting in Anand

Caste	Extent of electoral participation[38]	Congress	Lok Paksh
		%	%
Brahmins	A little more than half	90	10
Banias	Nearly two-thirds	80	20
Patidars	A little more than half	83	17
Kshatriyas	More than half	98	2

One of the interesting features of this observation was that proportionately more Kshatriyas were politically mobilised than Patidars, even though the rate of literacy and the need to protect private economic interests was higher among the Patidars. The caste-wise distribution of votes between the Congress Party and a regional opposition party (Lok Paksh), especially among the Patidars, was most striking, because of the influence exerted by a political party as opposed to a towering leader of the caste. The Lok Paksh had nominated Bhailalbhai Patel, possibly the greatest leader of the Patidars since Sardar Patel. In the constituency as a whole he secured a high percentage of the popular vote, but the Patidars of Anand did not give him more than 17 per cent of theirs. The Kshatriyas, like the other castes of Anand, overwhelmingly supported the Congress Party in India's first General Election, held in 1952.

The General Election of 1957, especially in the Kaira District, where Anand is located, took place against the background of two vital issues: a regional movement headed by the Mahagujarat Janata Parishad which demanded that a separate state of Gujarat be carved out of the composite state of Bombay; and the Land Tenancy Act, passed by the Congress government, which proposed handing over land ownership to the tenants. There were thus issues of regional sentiment and economic interest. The caste-wise performance of the parties was as shown in Table 2.3.

TABLE 2.3. The General Election of 1957: caste and voting in Anand

Caste	Extent of electoral Participation	Congress	Mahagujarat Janta Parishad Movement
		%	%
Brahmins	A little more than half	82	18
Banias	A little more than two-thirds	100	0
Patidars	More than two-thirds	61	39
Kshatriyas	More than two-thirds	100	0

The Banias, who had prospered with the growth of trade and commerce in Anand, felt indebted to the Congress Party and therefore fully switched their support to it. With the Patidars the Land Tenancy Act was an extremely unpopular measure. Some of the medium- and large-scale land-holders among them had either lost a part of their land or had felt threatened. At the other extreme, the Congress land-tenure policy was very popular with the Kshatriyas, who were either petty land-holders, tenants, or landless labourers. Being essentially the peasant castes of this area, the Patidars as well as the Kshatriyas were deeply affected by the changes in land-tenure policy despite the fact that Anand's agriculturist population had registered a downward trend as a result of the growth of commerce and industry there. During the General Election of 1957, therefore, the Patidar support for the Congress Party fell to below two-thirds, whereas that of the Kshatriyas rose to 100 per cent.

The 1962 General Election was marked in Anand by a bi-partisan contest of the two regionally well-balanced parties. The political opponents of the Congress Party had put together a new political entity with a distinct economic policy, political ideology, party organisation and leadership. This was the Swatantra Party. The seat of Gujarat Swatantra was and has been Vidyanagar, which is on the outskirts of Anand. Although the party had come into existence a short time before the General Election of 1962, serious differences among the regional groups within the Congress Party and a number of economic issues, including the Land Tenancy Act, helped the new party to mobilise political support. In Anand the distribution of the party vote caste-wise was as shown in Table 2.4.

TABLE 2.4. The General Election of 1962: caste and voting in Anand

Caste	Extent of electoral participation	Congress	Swatantra
		%	%
Brahmins	More than three-fourths	64	36
Banias	More than three-fourths	64	36
Patidars	About three-fourths	37	63
Kshatriyas	More than three-fourths	85	15

The Brahmin, and more so the Bania, support for the Congress Party declined considerably in 1962. The economic policies of the Swatantra Party proved to be quite attractive to both these castes. Some Brahmins and a great many Banias were in the grain trade and were petty shopkeepers. To them the increasing restrictions placed on economic activity by the Congress's ideology and its policies of socialism were most irksome. The Swatantra ideology of unrestricted trade and commerce, on the other hand, was particularly attractive.

The caste which was most strongly drawn to the Swatantra Party ideology was that of the Patidars. At last they had found a party which suited their innovative, pragmatic and result-oriented approach to economic life. Swatantra's economic philosophy had everything that such an industrious and economically successful caste was looking for. Moreover, the Swatantra leadership was locally based (i.e. in Vidyanagar), which offered the additional possibility of influencing its organisation and decision making.

The most interesting feature of the Patidar vote for the Swatantra Party was in the fact that it was given to the party as such rather than to the candidate. For the Swatantra Party had nominated a Kshatriya candidate, while the Congress Party had chosen a Patidar candidate. Yet for the Patidars of Anand, the appeal of the candidate's caste proved to be weaker than that of party ideology.

The same was true of the Kshatriya vote. Even though the Kshatriya Sabha had electorally aligned itself with the Swatantra Party, and had mobilised its entire machinery and resources to fighting the campaign, as well as backing a leading Kshatriya candidate, nevertheless the Kshatriyas of Anand overwhelmingly voted for the Congress Party and its Patidar candidate. The Congress policy of giving protection to the poorer section of the agriculturists and its general pro-underdog image had a special attraction for them.

The General Election of 1962 in Anand, from the point of view of caste and democratic politics, was therefore most significant: It brought about a polarisation of vote on ideological and programmatic lines that cut across the social cleavages of castes. Both Congress Party and the Swatantra Party had political support among all the four major castes, and, what is more, neither candidate succeeded in attracting all the votes of the caste he represented. To top it all, even the 'caste association', in this case the Kshatriya Sabha, could not succeed in shepherding the Kshatriya voters in the direction of its candidate. Along with a differentiated vote in their ranks, the Kshatriyas were engaged in questioning the leadership and political direction given by their 'caste association'.

The General Election of 1962 was also a watershed in the development of secularism in the politics of Anand. It saw the diversification of political support for both the parties not only in terms of castes, but also with reference to the two religious minorities, the Christians and the Muslims. Both these minorities had given their *en bloc* support to the Congress Party in the General Elections of 1952 and 1957. Their anxieties about the secular future of the Indian republic had evoked, in the past, an undifferentiated support for the Congress Party, which was more explicitly committed to secularism than most other parties. A decade after the birth of the Indian republic, and after two General Elections, the Christians first and then the Muslims acquired sufficient confidence in India's secular future to be able to diversify their democratic choice. Not being involved in religious problems, which had led to the partition of India in 1947, the Christians were the first to gain enough confidence to exercise their choice clearly. The Muslims were not far behind. The distribution of party votes in terms of minorities was as set out in Table 2.5.

TABLE 2.5. The General Election of 1962: religious minorities and voting in Anand

Religious minorities	Extent of electoral participation	Congress	Swatantra
		%	%
Christians	More than three-fourths	75	25
Muslims	Nearly three-fourths	89	11

The General Election of 1967 witnessed continued diversification in the political base of the Congress and Swatantra Parties among the castes and the religious minorities of Anand. Their share of the popular vote in terms of caste and religious minorities is shown in Table 2.6.

TABLE 2.6. The General Election of 1967: caste, religious minorities and voting in Anand

Caste and religious minorities	Congress	Swatantra
	%	%
Brahmins	36	64
Banias	21	79
Patidars	23	77
Kshatriyas	84	16
Christians	74	26
Muslims	79	21

For the election of 1967, the Congress Party had nominated two Kshatriya leaders for the parliamentary and Assembly seats, and the Swatantra party had chosen a well-known, ICS-(Indian Civil Service) retired Patidar leader for both the seats. There was a fierce struggle for the Kshatriya vote. While the Kshatriya Sabha had come out in favour of the Swatantra party, the local Congress leaders had helped towards the establishment of a rival Kshatriya body called the Kshatriya Seva Samaj.

The period between 1962 and 1967 in India was marked by a phenomenal rise in the cost of living, increased complaints about bureaucratic slowness and excessive restrictions, and the visible new prosperity largely confined to men in industry, commerce, bureaucracy and politics. Ironically enough, the people who had prospered most during the Congress regime – Brahmins, Banias and Patidars – were looking for an alternative government, while among the Kshatriyas, who had experienced only a trickle of prosperity, few were not looking for a change in party rule. The Congress Party had lost supporters across the board, including some Kshatriyas. Its greatest losses were among the Banias, then among Brahmins, and finally among the Patidars. The fall in its popularity among the Kshatriyas was very slight, but was there, nevertheless. What was significant in their case was that a well-known Kshatriya leader, Narendra Singh Mahida, who had gone over to the Swatantra[39] in the 1962 election and had subsequently returned to the Congress fold before the 1967 election, could not, along with a Kshatriya running mate for the Assembly seat, pull more votes for the Congress Party. This had occurred in spite of the fact that the local Congress leaders were instrumental in establishing the rival Kshatriya body Seva Samaj.

The emergence of a non-Congress vote among the Christians and the Muslims was also most significant. The decline in Congress popularity among the Muslims in the 1967 election was considerable. While the diversity in the Christian and Muslim vote indicated a growing confidence in the secular character of political parties, there were certain additional local reasons for the disaffection with the Congress Party. A group of the Christians in Anand had had a raw deal at the hands of the local Congress bosses in connection with the closing of the hospital they ran, and thus prompted some of the Christians to try an alternative to the Congress Party. As far as the Muslims were concerned, a sub-group, the Vohras, which engaged in the grain trade and other commercial ventures, had developed professional concern about the restrictive Congress policy in matters of trade in general. The economic interests of the Vohras had induced them to identify themselves with the others in their profession. Since the bulk of the grain traders favoured Swatantra ideology, the Vohras went along with them.

In the General Election of 1971 the trend towards declining political homogeneity among castes and religious communities of Anand continued. As in all other previous General Elections in Anand, the 1967 contest was almost entirely a battle between two political groups – this time between the two factions of the old Congress Party, the Ruling Congress headed by Mrs Gandhi, and the Organisation Congress led in Gujarat by Morarji Desai. Both the parties had nominated Kshatriya candidates.

The people of Anand were initially inclined to view the election of 1971 as a contest between the two Kshatriyas. But their attitude subsequently changed when the regional newspapers on both sides started playing up the themes of political stability, economic development, employment, price control, fair distribution of income, etc. On top of that came the campaign visit of Mrs Gandhi, for which more than 100,000 persons turned out from within a radius of about forty miles. Her meeting was disrupted by the agents of the Organisation Congress, a disruption that adversely affected the following of the Organisation Congress in Anand. More and more criticism was voiced against its tactics and its electoral alliance with three such ideologically diverse parties as the Swatantra, the Jan Sangh, and the SSP. It would therefore not be an exaggeration to say that the election of 1971 in Anand took place in an atmosphere of near-breakdown of party machinery on both sides. The Ruling Congress Party had utilised the charismatic appeal and the pro-underdog image of Mrs Gandhi. The organisation Congress Party, on the other hand, had relied heavily on personal influence and pressure, terror tactics, etc., to get a favourable response. Nevertheless in terms of caste and religious communities the performance of the two sides was as set out in Table 2.7.

The support of the Organisation Congress among the Brahmins, Banias, Patidars, and Christians was most impressive. Its support among the Kshatriyas was greater than that received by the Swatantra Party in the two previous general elections. Its support among the Muslim voters, too, was impressive, largely because one of its electoral allies was the extreme-right-wing Jan Sangh Party, and also because the election had taken place in an atmosphere of communal tension in the cities of Gujarat. The most impressive support for the Organisation Congress had come from the Patidars,

TABLE 2.7.   The General Election of 1971: caste, religious minorities and voting
in Anand

Caste and religious minorities	Ruling Congress	Organisation Congress
	%	%
Brahmins	23	77
Banias	29	71
Patidars	10	90
Kshatriyas	76	24
Christians	33	67
Muslims	63	37

who had identified themselves with it enthusiastically.

The Ruling Congress, on the other hand, had clearly introduced into Indian electoral politics a specific economic appeal which was comprehensible to the average voter. As Mrs Gandhi herself repeated in her various campaign speeches, her policy was not to take away people's prosperity but to generate new wealth which could reach the poor. Earlier her policy of nationalising the banks, which had proved a great blessing to the small borrower, had established her credentials in the eyes of the lower-income group. To the needy and the poor, therefore, the Ruling Congress was the party of the underdog. To the middle class and to businessmen her party held out the hope of political stability, which a motley assemblage of parties like the Organisation Congress and its allies, as experience in other states showed, did not.

While the ratio of popular vote between the Ruling Congress and the Organisation Congress among our six groups was 3:4 it was not so wide among the lower strata of society, which had narrowed the margin of the Organisation Congress.

The election of 1972 could not have been more opportune for the Ruling Congress, whose landslide victory in the previous election not only provided political stability to India but also restored confidence in its democratic future. The architect of that victory was Mrs Gandhi, who in the eyes of the average voter rose to great heights at the time of crisis. Her rise to prominence meant that the Indian democracy no longer needed extraordinary men like Nehru to run it. It meant that even a person like Mrs Gandhi, whose capacity for leadership and political skill had only recently been put to the test could rise to the occasion when faced with a challenge.

What she gave the average voter was a touch of self-assurance. Moreover, her timing and handling of the Bangladesh crisis electrified the country. On the eve of the 1972 election, therefore, there was no doubt about which party would win the bulk of the Indian states which had gone to the polls. Most of the guessing around election time was about how large the victory of Mrs Gandhi's party would be.

Unlike the elections in the past, the 1972 election in Anand saw three political parties in the fray: the Ruling Congress Party, the Organisation Congress Party and the Jan Sangh Party. The two Congress Parties had pitted against each other two young Kshatriyas, both of humble birth, of almost equal age, both from the same village, and even distantly related. While the nominee of the Ruling Congress was the more educated, that of the Organisation Congress had the advantage of having been a member of the dissolved Assembly. The Jan Sangh, on the other hand, had nominated a young Patidar. Table 2.8 shows the response to the three political parties in the election of 1972.

TABLE 2.8. The Assembly election of 1972: caste, religious minorities and voting in Anand

Caste and religious minorities	Ruling Congress	Organisation Congress	Jan Sangh
	%	%	%
Brahmins	54	38	8
Banias	45	30	25
Patidars	38	37	25
Kshatriyas	74	24	2
Christians	67	28	5
Muslims	67	30	3

The Ruling Congress had greatly improved its position and its support from all groups except the Kshatriyas. Among the Kshatriyas the declining trend in support for the Ruling Congress had continued, and such Kshatriya vote as it got was largely for the party rather than the candidate. The Patidars, instead of supporting the Patidar candidate nominated by the Jan Sangh gave three-quarters of their votes to the two Kshatriya candidates nominated by the two Congress parties. All the six major groups of Anand diversified their votes. Even the two religious minorities gave some support to a traditionalist party such as the Jan Sangh.

The Assembly election of 1975 was held in an atmosphere of intense debate following what was popularly known as the Navnirman Movement, which exercised pressures on elected deputies to resign and thereby toppled the then Congress Party-dominated government of Gujarat. The debate concerned an unprecedented problem in Indian politics, namely what ought an electorate to do when it is convinced that its elected deputies no longer work for the welfare of the people. Should it allow those deputies to complete their normal term of office or recall them by means of political agitation and direct pressure generated by launching *satyagraha*? While the debate was in progress all over the country the Navnirman Movement succeeded in forcing New Delhi to call for a fresh Assembly election. The campaign speeches preceding the election underlined some of these questions.

As far as Anand was concerned, the secular character of the Navnirman Movement was undermined by the traditional ethnic hostility between the Brahmins, Banias and Patidars on the one hand, and the Kshatriyas on the other. The ethnic conflict was activated by the desperate local Congress Organisation which wanted to use its base among Kshatriyas to counter the Navnirman Movement. Joint attempts were made by Patidar and Kshatriya youths but without success.

In the electoral fray of 1975, there were three political parties: the Congress Party, the Janata Party, and the Kisan Majdoor Lok Paksh Party (KMLP). The last one was started by Chimanbhai Patel, who had been Chief Minister but was thrown out of office by the movement and later on by the Congress Party itself.

Since the youth of Gujarat had actively participated in the Navnirman Movement and subsequently in the election campaign, we shall consider their electoral choices separately.

Table 2.9 shows the distribution of votes of the majority of voters in Anand.

Among the Brahmins the appeal of the Congress Party had dwindled considerably. The majority were engaged in white-collar jobs and their wages had not kept pace with the phenomenal rise in the cost of living. In contrast, among the Banias and the Patidars substantial numbers were engaged in trade and commerce, and had benefited by the soaring prices. The majority of the Kshatriyas pinned their continuing hope for better days on the policies of the Congress Party. Finally, as far as the Christians and the Muslims

TABLE 2.9. The Assembly election of 1975: caste, religious minorities and voting in Anand

Caste and religious minorities	Congress	Janata	KMLP
	%	%	%
Brahmins	24	72	4
Banias	40	55	5
Patidars	36	42	22
Kshatriyas	77	21	2
Christians	63	37	–
Muslims	78	19	3

were concerned, the intensive propaganda on the part of the Congress Party that its defeat would seriously jeopardise freedom of conscience, had less effect than before. In all previous elections, the Congress Party had successfully exploited this issue. By 1975, the issue very nearly ran its course as one-third of the Christians and one-fifth of the Muslims voted for the Janata, knowing full well that one of its constituent elements was the traditionalist, Jan Sangh Party. See Table 2.10.

TABLE 2.10. The Assembly election of 1975: caste, religious minorities (youth) and voting in Anand

Caste and religious minorities	Congress	Janata	KMLP
	%	%	%
Brahmins	15	57	28
Banias	20	43	37
Patidars	22	65	13
Kshatriyas	93	7	–
Christians	80	20	–
Muslims	90	10	–

The Brahmin, Bania, and Patidar youth did not support the Congress Party in any great number, but favoured the Janata instead. But Kshatriya youth backed the Congress Party in a big way, partly because of the hope that it would solve their unemployment problem. The same was true of the younger Christians and Muslims, who saw their chances of being employed in various public undertakings as being decidedly better than elsewhere.

The election of 1977 was held in an atmosphere of fear, electoral unpreparedness and a suspicion that the Congress Party would continue in power whatever the result. Although after the Navnirman Movement the Janata group was given the mandate to constitute the government in Gujarat the declaration of a state of emergency in June 1975 had introduced a period of great uncertainty. The people of Gujarat were not very sure how long Mrs Gandhi, with all the extraordinary powers at her command, would tolerate another political group in power. Soon after imprisoning the leaders of several parties which had asked for her resignation, Mrs Gandhi strongly emphasised the themes of national security, law and order, discipline and the need to check economic crimes. The detention of smugglers and black marketeers, the banning of strikes and the general atmosphere of discipline were initially welcomed by the people of Anand. But soon it became evident that the extraordinary powers were going to be used against all political dissidents regardless of whether or not they were involved in political agitation.

A week before the announcement of the election of 1977, the rumours of an impending election had started to circulate. When the announcement was actually made there was an atmosphere of disbelief. When the statements of opposition leaders like Morarji Desai and J. P. (Jayaprakash Narayan) were printed by the newspapers the atmosphere started changing. Nevertheless, the people of Anand were still not sure why Mrs Gandhi, who appeared to be firmly in command, had called the election. For them there were two possible outcomes of the election: first, that with vast resources at her command she would win the elections hands down and thereby legitimise whatever she had done in the past; second, in the unlikely event of the electoral result going against her and her party, she might stage-manage riots and violence and thereby claim that the people of India were not yet ready to resume the democratic process. In either case, they thought, she and her men would be back.

Consequently, because of the atmosphere of fear and uncertainty, my research assistants and I could not get the kind of co-operation from our respondents that we had hitherto enjoyed. Table 2.11 shows the distribution of votes between the Congress and the Janata Parties among as many respondents as were willing to divulge their voting intentions to us.

TABLE 2.11.   The General Election of 1977: caste, religious minorities and voting in Anand

Caste and religious minorities	Congress	Janata
Brahmins (%)	–	100
Banias (%)	–	100
Patidars (%)	5	95
Kshatriyas (%)	79	21
Christians	Less than two-thirds	More than one-third
Muslims	Less than one-fourth	More than three-quarters

The Brahmins, the Banias and the Patidars were deeply influenced by the possibility of building a strong opposition to the
Congress Party, if not dislodging it from power. As newspapers
reported the extent of resentment among the people of India against
corruption, the high-handedness of officials and the financial
irregularities of Sanjay Gandhi, more and more people from these
three groups decided to make a determined effort to register their
anger against the party. So far as the Kshatriyas were concerned
their leaders presented the election as a moment of crisis for Mrs
Gandhi and therefore as Kshatriyas (warriors) they must stand by
her side rather than desert her. The younger segment among them,
however, needed great persuasion before they would support the
Congress Party.

The Christians and the Muslims continued their search for a
political alternative to the Congress Party despite the talk about
their possible loss of freedom of conscience under a non-Congress
Party government.

Finally, it is instructive to note the pattern of popular support for
the Congress Party among the Kshatriyas. From 1962 to 1972, the
period when a diversification occurred in the Kshatriya vote,
despite the presence or absence of a Kshatriya candidate or
candidates, or an electoral brief for or against from the Kshatriya
Sabha or Kshatriya Seva Samaj, the majority of Kshatriyas
continued to support the Congress Party. Over the years, however,
their support for the party steadily declined. Neither the presence of
a caste candidate nor a brief from a 'caste association' could check
it.

VI FRAGMENTATION OF THE DECISION-MAKING UNITS

In the final analysis any attempt at grasping the relationship between caste and politics in contemporary India takes us back to the problem identified by Srinivas, that during the Pax Britannica individual castes achieved horizontal integration at the social level. So far as their politics are concerned, in my view, a reverse process is very much in evidence. Political cohesion of the castes, wherever present, is in the process of shrinking from the wider horizontal integrations to smaller and more diversified residential segments.

What the decade under review here witnessed was the growing reluctance on the part of all the social groups to let ethnic or religious considerations get mixed up with the problem of political choice. Economically backward groups took longer to arrive at such a position, but in exercising political choice they were inhibited more by their insecurity than by the inborn compulsions of their ethnicity. The insecurity of the religious minorities and its consequent effect on their political choice was further reinforced by the problem of religion. But in both cases the search for political alternative to the Congress Party, however limited, was accompanied by confidence that change would not reintroduce setbacks and that the concern for the poor and secularism would gain strength no matter which party came to power.

3 The Three Electoral Generations

Unlike the relatively more evolved political culture of Western democracies, the Indian democratic phenomenon is still very much on the anvil. In shaping it, the traditional norms of private and public conduct have played as great a part as the egalitarian norms implicit in democratic ideology. Moreover, the different age-groups, influenced by circumstances prevailing during their entry into the labour force and the acquisition of voting status, tend to adopt differentiated perspectives and standards in evaluating the conduct of men in public life and the performance of institutions, and in the identification of issues. Such perspectives and standards reflect a blend of the traditional and democratic norms on the one hand, and the imprints of the formative years of various generations on the other. In this chapter I shall make use of the concept of generations in order to throw light on the different generational perspectives on the functioning of democratic institutions in India.

I THE CONCEPT OF GENERATIONS

Various studies on elections in India, Britain, and the USA, while examining the relationship between the vote and age, have either avoided or paid insufficient attention to the concept of generations. In their cohort analysis they tend to restrict themselves, by and large, to the specific attitudes of certain age-groups, rather than relating such attitudes to the historical circumstances which conditioned them. Thus, for example, in their seminal study *Political Change in Britain*, Butler and Stokes refrained from using the concept of generations and showed a preference for the notion of 'political life-cycle',[1] which presumably involves as much 'licence' on their part as the use of the concept of generations might have done. The notion of 'political life-cycle' is used by Butler and Stokes to describe 'political man' in the four phases of his development from innocence, awareness, interest in politics, and, finally, unchanging partisan allegiance.[2] Such a formulation no doubt helps the authors to consider the relationship between the vote and age against the background of family and class[3] on the one hand, and the length of partisan attachment on the other.[4] What is left out, however, regardless of the perspectives inherited or developed through the influences of family and class and the duration of partisan attachment, is the vital question of those commonly shared experiences of one's generation, *across* family and class, which as effectively condition one's political responses as do the other two.

The authors of *Voting*, one of the unexcelled works in the field, towards the very end of their study recognised the importance of the concept of generations. In their words:

> while it is true that we find generations to exist in politics (those who came of age in the 1920's being more Republican, those in the 1930's more Democratic), actually what is more marked in the data and more interesting is this: *that these generations differ markedly in the basis of their voting tradition.* The generation of the 1920's splits more on religion, that of the 1930's more on socio-economic class.[5]

In *Voting* Berelsen *et al* sought to overcome the deficiencies of their earlier work, *The People's Choice*, in which the average voter was mistakenly considered to be an isolated individual. Consequently, in *Voting* itself, too much attention is paid to the influence of primary groups in electoral opinion formation and relatively little to the forces of the environment. The environment is credited with influence only when it breaches through the primary groups, and is identified by the authors by means of a special name, the 'breakage' effect.[6] For Berelsen and his co-authors such a breach is possible only when the primary groups themselves are not politically homogeneous. What the authors omitted to do, therefore, was to examine the influence of contemporary forces on the age-cohorts across primary groups. Despite their identification of the political generations of the decades of the 1920s and 1930s, they did not identify groups with common exposure to historical circumstances for their intensive analysis.

This was done admirably by William M. Evan in his paper 'Cohort Analysis of Survey Data'.[7] Evan expressed his dissatisfaction at the restriction of cohort analysis to such themes as 'fertility', 'participation in labour force', 'occupation change', etc. As a tool of analysis, he thought, it could be used in analysing other areas, especially what he called the 'opinion change'. By correlating age-groups with historical circumstances, he felt, one could fruitfully undertake even generational analysis.[8]

Evan was in fact engaged in empirically testing the basic question raised by Karl Mannheim, of what in fact is the influence of 'change in historical circumstances' on a generation's entry into 'the occupational and political statuses of a society'.[9] Basically, then, his paper was an attempt to determine the relative influence of 'historical circumstances' as against other factors, including age, on a generation. For his own purposes, Evan closely examined the data collected by the American Institute of Public Opinion's survey of cohort groups in 1937 (the period of economic depression), 1945 (the war); and 1953 (post-war prosperity). During each survey an exact number of years was added on to identify the cohort groups which had temporally advanced. This was, then, a panel analogue of cohort groups for 're-interview' under the historical circumstances. Each time the same question was addressed: 'Do you believe that the government should buy, own, operate the railroads?' The changes in historical situation had indeed brought to the surface different responses. Evan finally reached the conclusion that 'age as compared with the historical factor has a relatively negligible effect on changes in opinion regarding government ownership of railroads'.[10]

The manner in which Evan tried to test Mannheim's thesis had its own difficulties. No matter how reliable one's sampling technique may be, the two different cohort groups, set apart by a certain number of years – with the older among the two also advancing in age – are not in actual fact one and the same cohort groups. To be able to arrive at a reliable inference on this crucial question there is no short cut, in my opinion, to the panel method whereby one re-interviews the *same* people over an extended period of time.

Despite such a shortcoming Evan opened up the possibility of empirically testing Mannheim's most vital sociological concept of generations. Before we consider specific aspects of this concept in the Indian situation it will be worth our while to examine the views of its foremost exponent, Karl Mannheim himself.

Mannheim tried to formulate his concept of generations from a sociological point of view. He rejected the positivist notion of generations, especially that of Comte, on the ground that it was too closely tied to a 'chronological'[11] table. Instead, he showed his preference for the esoteric notions of generations put forward by Dilthey ('the inner unity of a generation') and Heidegger ('togetherness in the same world, and the consequent preparedness for a distinct set of possibilities, determines the direction of individual destinies in advance'),[12] and set out to formulate his own concept based on their insights but at the same time one that could be used for more general sociological explanations. At the hands of Mannheim the concept of generations finally became a powerful tool of analysis, particularly in the case of societies which were undergoing rapid social change and/or registering consciously directed political changes, as in the case of India.

For Mannheim a generation is not a 'concrete group' such as a family, tribe, or a sect. Nor is it similar to a voluntary body. To some extent it resembles the phenomenon of class. Both class and generation require the 'location' of a number of individuals in a particular social and historical process.[13]

The fact of belonging to the same class or the same generation gives to the individuals in it certain common characteristic modes of thought and experience. But while the class phenomenon is explainable in terms of the difference in social and economic conditions, that of the generation becomes meaningful in terms of location or transition from one generation to another.

Both class and generation underline the contemporaneity.[14] But the concept of generation also has an additional dimension to it, namely, sequentiality. It is in its differential sequentiality that a generation self-consciously considers itself to be different from the others preceding it. While class as well as generation are phenomena which occur within the social and historical process, temporally speaking, generation embraces class. As a concept, generation would take into account the integrative forces together with the differentiating forces present in a time-span and would go out to identify the variety of life-styles, attitudes, normative dispositions and political expectations of sub-units within each generation. In the case of a class, on the other hand, because of the historical accretions in its special conceptual use, one would look for homogeneity of attitudes, and economic and political goals. Moreover, the concept of class, having been too frequently used in order to express the element of conflict among different categories involved in productive relations, has certain inclusion-exclusion characteristics to it, which is not the case with the concept of generation, within which even the fringes, borders and sub-generational units come to acquire socio-political significance of their own.

Unlike the Comtian notion of generations, which begins and ends with a chronological table, Mannheim emphasised the need to carve out a discrete generation unit on the basis of its already expressed socio-political peculiarities and then revert *back* to its temporal periodisation. At his hands, therefore, the notion of generation shifts from a mere time-span to revealed peculiarities within it. The social and causal analysis which can be undertaken with the help of the concept of generations can help us in relating and explaining the peculiarities of a generation in terms of the influences during its formative years. Most important among these are the influences during the period when the members of a generation enter the labour force and acquire political status as voters. Circumstances prevailing during the acquisition of the new economic and political status leave behind lasting impressions on one's norms, expectations and the understanding of social reality.

Mannheim made a distinction between 'generation location' and 'generation as an actuality'.[15] The latter for him was the product of 'a concrete bond . . . created between the members of a generation by their being exposed to the social and intellectual symptoms of a dynamic destabilization'.[16] In other words, a period of rapid social change is often instrumental in crystallising a group of people into discrete generations.[17]

The model provided by Mannheim for generation identification and analysis has the following three characteristics: the revealed peculiarities of cohort group; explanations of those peculiarities in terms of the dominant influences during its formative years; and the location of periods of destabilisation which separate one generation from another.

In the pages that follow I shall make use of Mannheim's model in order to locate and analyse the revealed peculiarities of what I have called the three electoral generations of India.

II THE THREE ELECTORAL GENERATIONS AND THE CONGRESS PARTY

The structural dimensions of Indian politics are often conceived too heavily in terms of the caste system. To some extent that is justified, but it is a factor that is often emphasised to the total exclusion of any others. So far, for instance, there has been no attempt made either to identify or to test the view that common exposure to prevailing circumstances to some extent leads to shared standpoints in viewing social and political realities. Nearly three decades have passed since India introduced democratic institutions, and the voters, who entered her electoral system at different times, have brought to bear different sets of perspectives and norms in judging the performance of those institutions. Such a time-span then should help us to identify the intra-generational diversity and the inter-generational shifts in viewing the performance of institutions based on de-mocratic ideology.

Originally, we had not prepared ourselves for a generational analysis of our data on the five elections. But while correlating the data on age and vote we were persuaded to look at our cohort analysis in terms of generations rather than mere age differentials. This then gave a much wider significance to electoral response and its antecedent reasoning on the part of the voters.

Until the parliamentary election of 1971, we could identify the two distinct electoral generations in Anand: those who were above and those who were below their middle-fifties. The former we shall term the 'old' generation and the latter the 'middle' generation. The old generation entered the democratic political system with a great deal of veneration for the sacrifices made by the political leaders during the struggle for Indian independence. Its political expectations were coloured by the ups and downs of the national movement and the ability and dedication of the average freedom-fighter who experienced it. Its normative expectation of the politician during the post-independence period was pitched very high. Finally, it remained an unrelenting critic of the falling standards of public life.

The middle generation, on the other hand, had enjoyed the full benefit of employment and the trickle of prosperity that came in the wake of Indian independence. Having been politically socialised into venerating the national leaders, it was also grateful for the relative improvement in its economic condition. During the moments of bitter criticism and disillusionment with the performance of the politicians, it had a slight economic cushion to fall back upon. Its attitude to the politicians, unlike that of the old generation, was flexible and pragmatic.

In 1971, however, there was the entry of still another electoral generation into the Indian political system.[18] This generation, which we shall call the 'young' generation, was wholly born in free India. Its political socialisation, especially as regards the veneration of the outstanding national leaders, was very limited indeed. What it had witnessed when it politically came of age, to its horror, was the widespread practice of political defection. It had been exposed to some of the shameless acts of the sale of political support for cash by some seasoned politicians. Such a phenomenon had conditioned the young generation into rejecting those political parties which did not emphasise personal qualities in politicians above everything else. Deeply influenced by its teachers and the people with whom it socially interacted, the majority in this generation developed a dislike for the Ruling Congress Party, which had attracted the maximum number of defectors to its rank.

For the purposes of our analysis we shall treat the old, the middle and the young as three distinct electoral generations. Each of them had its own characteristic political response, perception of issues and party preference.

Within the three electoral generations there was also an intra-generational difference. None of them was electorally or in terms of broader political questions completely homogeneous. On the contrary, like all other generations they too contained differentiated and sometimes antagonistic generation units. In the middle generation, in particular, a wide range of diversity was noticeable. At its two extremes the middle generation was sandwiched by the units which had a lot in common with the one preceding as well as the one following it. See Table 3.1.

In order to focus sharply on the revealed political peculiarities of the three electoral generations, we had selected the attitude to the Congress Party as the focal point of their political response. For all the three generations, the party had been either the most vital political experience or a vital political landmark. Having been at the centre of Indian politics for a little less than a century, there was a great deal in it for the people of all age groups to react to. The Congress Party had not only organised a massive movement for

TABLE 3.1.   Age cohorts within the three electoral generations

Age-groups	Electoral generation	Age identified in
55–64 yrs	Old generation	1966–7
(i) 45–54 yrs (ii) 35–44 yrs (iii) 25–34 yrs (iv) 21–24 yrs	Middle generation	1966–7
First-time voters	Young generation	1971

independence on a scale unknown in human history but had also
consolidated the fruits of independence by means of a secular,
democratic political system. Furthermore, it had tried to force the
pace of social change despite an inconceivable number of odds. In
its drive towards all these objectives, it had gained, sustained and
lost its supporters. The Congress Party, therefore, was the adequate
focal-point for getting an insight into the different political
responses of the three electoral generations.

During the elections of 1967 and 1971, the voters were offered two
major choices: the Congress Party (united) and the Swatantra
Party; and the Ruling Congress and the Organisation Congress.
During the election of 1972, however, the contest was triangular:
between the Ruling Congress; the Organisation Congress; and the
Jan Sangh. In terms of their ideology, party programme and
implicit social direction, one could make the following classification
in relative terms, as shown in Table 3.2.

TABLE 3.2.   Election and party ideology

Year of election	Left	Right	Further right
1967	Congress (united)	Swatantra	–
1971	The Ruling Congress	The Organisation Congress	–
1972	The Ruling Congress	The Organisation Congress	The Jan Sangh

Of all the age cohorts, the men in the age-group 55–64 were fully
exposed to the influence created by the heroism and dedication of
the leaders of the Congress Party who fought for Indian inde-

pendence. This was also the generation which had experienced such joy at the coming of Indian independence. The self-sacrifice and, in certain cases, the moral qualities of the top-ranking leaders had left a deep impression on this generation. It was therefore inclined to evaluate the performance of the average Congress leader with reference to the high standard of service and dedication set up by the front-ranking leaders of the Congress Party before and soon after independence. There was also an element of severity in its political judgement which, as time went by, acquired the quality of irreversibility. That is to say, the old generation electorate did not make any allowance for the weaknesses of politicians in public life nor indeed for their inability to achieve promised results. Over the years their support for the Congress Party, an organisation which they had deeply cherished in the past, continually dwindled, and by 1972 not even one-third of the voters among them were willing to back it. The gradual political alienation of this generation from the Congress Party was reflected in its vote: 1967 (44 per cent); 1971 (36 per cent); and 1972 (32 per cent).

The continual erosion of support for the Congress Party among the old generation was not due to the party's increasingly left-wing stance, but, as the voters across various groups within this generation pointed out, because of the corrupt practices encouraged or condoned by the Congress government. The judgement of this generation, as it emerged through its vote, was not so much on the political performance as on the public conduct of the men in office.

The electoral generation which comprised the various middle-aged cohorts had its own sub-units expressing a variety of concerns and presenting a heterogeneous electoral image. At its two extremes, as stated earlier, its oldest and youngest sub-units even shared the political outlook of the generations that preceded or followed them.

The oldest sub-unit of the middle generation, 45–54 years of age, shared the political judgement and anxiety of the old generation especially in matters of the decline in the tone of public life in the 1960s. But unlike the men in the old generation, the voters in this age cohort were much less inflexible in their political judgement. The growing trend of antipathy towards the Congress Party in this age-group, therefore, was not irreversible. Over the years its support for the party was as follows: 1967 (47 per cent); 1971 (31 per cent); and 1972 (56 per cent).

Its votes for the Congress Party registered great swings. Especially after 1971, it was willing to give another chance to the Ruling Congress to do something to arrest the falling standards of public life. Its support for the Congress Party, which dramatically increased in 1972, pinned its hopes on the firm leadership of Mrs Gandhi.

The second segment within the middle generation, in the age-group 35–44, was, politically speaking, a sedate group. Over the years its party identification remained unchanged: 1967 (54 per cent); 1971 (58 per cent); and 1972 (54 per cent).

The people in this age cohort were in their middle teens and twenties when India attained her independence. The youngest among them were enfranchised a decade ago and the oldest among them had participated as voters in India's first General Election. This age-group was deeply influenced by Nehru, Patel and other national leaders. It had also shared their confidence in India's democratic future and their excitement at the task of her social reconstruction. Its memory of the initial excitement survived the subsequent trials and tribulations. Economically, too, this age-group had benefited the most as a result of the increased employment and business opportunities that came in the wake of independence.

This, then, was the age-group which was the mainstay of the Congress Party as a political organisation. As long as the party produced leaders of the calibre of Nehru, Patel and Mrs Gandhi, professed an ideology of social welfare, introduced public ownership in the crucial areas of the economy, imposed heavy taxes on the rich, introduced enlightened policy towards a fair-sized land-holding, introduced relief measures whenever necessary, and allowed private enterprise in large-, medium- and small-scale business and industry, this age-group would continue to identify itself with the political organisation.

The voters in the age-group 25–34 shared the political responses not of the group immediately preceding it but the one before that. Instead of emulating the sedate 35–44-year-olds, it seemed to be under the influence of a possible parental group of 45–54 years of age. Over the years its support for the Congress Party ran parallel to the support registered by the parental group: 1967 (48 per cent); 1971 (32 per cent); and 1972 (47 per cent).

Lastly, within the middle generation, we come to the youngest segment, the age-group of 21–24 years. It came of electoral age at the very end of a political era, and, in a sense, stood at the generational divide.

The group was inducted into the democratic political system at the time when the split in the Congress Party and the consequent chaos in various legislative bodies was still a few years away. In 1967, when this age-group exercised its franchise for the first time, there were factional disputes within the Congress Party but no sign of the split.

The youngest segment in the middle generation continued to support the party with less than half of its electoral strength from 1967 to 1971, and in 1972 it even increased it.

What disassociated this segment from the one that followed it, was the formative influence of the period when it was enfranchised. It bore the imprint of a period which prized political stability more than the chancy political alternatives.

Finally, the young electoral generation. Having been inducted into the electoral system in 1971, at a time of disarray of party organisations in India, the first-time voters of the 1971 election reflected political anxieties of a different sort. The irreconcilable cleavages within the Congress Party, and opportunistic coalitions in various states, together with the cynical political defections for money and office represented about the gloomiest picture of Indian politics since independence. At the centre of it all, from the point of view of the young generation, were the corrupt, power-hungry and self-seeking politicians, of whom there seemed to be more in the Congress Party than anywhere else. This age-group therefore started looking for a political alternative which would emphasise the qualities of honesty, dedication and self-sacrifice in would-be politicians. To the young generation, especially in 1971 and 1972, the Jan Sangh appeared to be the political party which placed a high premium on those values. Encouraged in that direction by their college teachers, employers and colleagues, the first-time voters registered a large anti-Congress Party vote in 1971, and a pro-Jan Sangh and pro-Organisation Congress vote in 1972. The Ruling Congress Party received less than one-third of the votes of the young generation during the elections of 1971 and 1972.

It will be seen, then, that the three electoral generations in their attitude to the Congress Party displayed the unmistakable influence

74   *Democratic Process in a Developing Society*

of the periods in which they came of age. Their views on the performance of political organisations and the norms of public conduct were conditioned by the instances of firm commitment to moral values, the philosophies of social change and distributive justice and the need to guard against falling standards in public life. In the case of all the three electoral generations the abstract ideological principles of social and political life prevailing at the time of their coming of age proved far more effective than might have been thought possible.

Like anywhere else in the world the three electoral generations, old, middle and young, displayed the basic characteristics of withdrawal, persistence and change, respectively. Over the years, due to frustration and disillusionment with the performance of the Congress Party, the old generation gradually withdrew its support without going in search of a political alternative. Its increasing political marginality was in conformity with the traditional life-cycle of the Indians, in which the prime of life is followed by a gradual withdrawal from worldly concerns.

The middle generation, as a result of the orientation received from their own norms and expectations, was inclined to uphold the persistence of the Congress Party as a political organisation. Unlike the old and the young generations it was prepared to view the party's failures against the background of its achievements. It was much more inclined to underline the basic soundness of Congress Party policy and, despite its dubious implementation, was confident that before long the expected benefits would follow therefrom. To some extent it had achieved 'immunisation'[19] to the climate of critical opinion which engulfed it from all sides.

The young generation remained unimpressed by the Congress Party policy statements as such. What it looked for was the quality of the men implementing them. In its critical approach to the Congress Party, it lost sight of the importance of public policy and instead heavily underlined the personal qualities of the politicians. Such an orientation facilitated its drift towards the right-wing political parties.

Finally, the theoretical controversy surrounding the concepts of generation and maturation raised by Neal Cutler in his 'Generation, Maturation, and Party Affiliation: A Cohort Analysis'. The central question posed by the paper was whether the people of a generation continue to reflect the imprint of their formative years or grow out of it as the time passes. Neither the old nor the middle generation, while judging the performance of the Congress Party, deviated from their orientation of formative periods. Such an orientation continued, as this longitudinal analysis has indicated, over the years. As to the basic question of whether people become more conservative or not politically as they grow older, I shall examine this in the next section using the senescence hypothesis.

III   THE SENESCENCE HYPOTHESIS

In their *Political Change in Great Britain*, Butler and Stokes questioned, to some extent, what is often known as the senescence hypothesis. 'Both academics and journalists have thought,' they maintained, 'that many voters begin their political lives on the left and move rightward as they grow older.'[20] The senescence hypothesis, despite 'the weight of research' against it, to use Robert MacKenzie's apt phrase, has survived. A quarter of a century's painstaking research into voting behaviour, across cultural conditions, has not been able to put it to rest. At the height of the radicalism and restlessness of campus youth in the late 1960s, S. M. Lipset came out with a stunning remark: 'even in the countries where leftist demonstrations have made international headlines', the bulk of the youth 'tends to endorse moderate or even conservative parties'.[21]

The authors of *The People's Choice* make an incisive distinction between social and political conservatism. 'Advancing age', they say, 'may not bring *political* conservatism but it does bring *social* conservatism.'[22] Our findings, too, supported this distinction. The bulk of the young generation, as I will show in this section, were politically to the right of their own elders. For instance, while the middle generation, during the elections of 1971 and 1972 voted for strong central and state governments which could effectively implement some part of the socialist programme of the Ruling Congress, the young generation went in search of 'honest' politicians, no matter what their programmes might be. The voters in the young generation were not attracted so much to the concept of social justice implicit in the Congress Party programme, and the need to implement it effectively, as to the 'clean' background of the untried politicians put forward by the right-wing Jan Sangh or the splinter-group Organisation Congress.

Between the election of 1971 and 1972, the Ruling Congress made enormous gains in its political support from the middle generation. During the same period its hold on the young generation declined considerably. Within the votes cast by all the three generations, the Jan Sangh attracted, proportionately speaking, a greater slice of the support of the young generation than of the other two.

The search for 'honest' politicians led the youthful voters to try out the political alternative offered by the Jan Sangh. For its part, the Jan Sangh also emphasised the need for the *sadhu* (holy man) type of politician, who would be selfless, dedicated and disciplined. In his fascinating paper on Indian youth, Edward Shils wrote: 'The path of the *sadhu* is still trodden by a few but its traces beckon to many minds. The path of the resistant to the British rule was a variant of the *sadhu*'s path, and it was trodden by many, and for a long time . . .'[23]

By clever political salesmanship the Jan Sangh presented a *sadhu*-type image of its political workers and nominees and thereby succeeded in creating a soft corner for itself in the young generation. Coupled with this was the Jan Sangh's success in enlisting the sympathies of some college faculties, through which it exercised its influence on campus youth.

The senescence hypothesis thus does not get much support so far as our data are concerned. As a matter of fact it is difficult to find published research anywhere which supports the hypothesis.

IV   THE GENERATIONAL PERCEPTION OF ISSUES
     AND THE BLAME FOR HARDSHIPS

The three generations did not perceive national problems altogether differently. In most cases, on the other hand, there were differences in emphases and priorities, but sometimes their attempts to identify specific problems were closely linked with certain historical processes which not only made them discrete groups but also conditioned them to view common problems differently.

On the eve of the election of 1967, concern over a variety of issues was expressed by the various age cohorts in the middle generation as well as by the old generation. In this respect the middle generation itself was split into two parts: those below and those above thirty-five years of age. To the younger segment in the middle generation food shortages, the rapidly rising cost of living and widespread corruption needed urgent attention. The older segment, on the other hand endorsed these concerns but its wider experience of Indian problems persuaded it to add two more: defence and family planning. For it the problems of firmly securing India's borders and/ or reducing the size of the average family were no longer academic problems.

There was also a significant difference in the style of identifying issues. The younger segment of the middle generation expressed concern over the various issues in terms of how they affected them personally. The presentation of the same set of issues by the older segment of the same generation, on the other hand, remained much more impersonal and even dispassionate. The younger segment wanted open discussion and pinpointed political accountability on various issues. The older segment, on the other hand, put great faith in the rulers giving a better account of themselves once they knew how dissatisfied the public was.

So far as the old generation was concerned it was more or less resigned to the ineffectiveness of political action to solve major problems. For it the most urgent problems were food shortages and the cost of living, but given the *niti* (morality) of the Ministers and the officials, it maintained, not much could be expected from the politicians.

Four years later, on the eve of the election of 1971, across three generations, a great deal of concern was expressed over the vital problems facing the country, namely the rapidly rising cost of living, corruption and the rapid growth of population, usually in that order.

In all the social groups the severest critics of Congress Party policies, which had resulted in the rise in the cost of living, were those who were bringing up young families or had children of marriageable age. There was a heavy concentration of such critics in the age cohort 24–44 years.

Across all the generations there was concern over the rapid increase in population. This concern, however, was not so high in the young generation, was high in the middle, and then tapered off in the old.

People in the middle generation were naturally concerned with the problem of maintaining big families. The young generation, having just about started family life, were therefore a few years away from its economic pinching. Similarly, those belonging to the old generation had left family concerns behind them.

A year later, on the eve of the election of 1972, among the three major concerns of the previous year – i.e. the cost of living, population and corruption – the concern over corruption became secondary. This was partly due to the fact that Mrs Gandhi had acquired a reputation for firmness, and voters in all age cohorts took it for granted that she would deal firmly with those engaged in corrupt practices. The concern over the cost of living became a little less pronounced. But what became a matter of less than secondary importance was the problem of population. Being largely a collective rather than a personal problem, it easily faded into the background across all the age-groups. Later on, the population problem, unhappily, got entangled with the religious controversies among the Muslims. Their lack of enthusiasm for family planning quickly affected the Hindus. The rightist parties exploited the fears of the Hindus that one day they would be outnumbered by the Muslims. Consequently, across all age-groups much less anxiety was expressed over population expansion than during the previous years.

The problems of corruption and overpopulation were pushed aside by the concern over unemployment and poverty. The young generation, having freshly entered the labour force, remained most concerned with unemployment, the middle generation moderately concerned, and the old, as might be expected, the least.

During the years 1975–7,[24] poverty, population and the rising cost of living were identified as the major problems by the middle and old generation. So far as the cost of living was concerned it was often treated as a function of corruption. The young generation also subscribed to this view, except that in its case the cost of living, and the causal factor behind it – corruption – needed the most urgent attention. The mass protest in Gujarat had fully sensitised all the three groups to the problem of corruption.

While unemployment as a problem across all social groups had a horizontal spread, the problem of poverty came to acquire the vertical character of the social organisation. The emphasis on poverty as a major problem was less in the three upper strata – the Brahmins, Banias and Patidars – and greater among the Kshatriyas, Christians and Muslims who comprised the three lower strata of Anand Society.

This brings us to the problem of apportioning blame for the hardships endured by the three generations. The decade of the 1960s in India was one of indescribable hardship for the average man. During the period the cost of living rose phenomenally and, as always, kept abreast with the rise in wages. The growth of commerce and the expansion of industries in Anand, the pace of which was much faster than in other parts of India, did not create sufficient jobs for the school-leavers and urban migrants. Consequently, unemployment remained a perennial problem. The very poor, the poor and the hard-hit lower middle-class, who together constituted the bulk of Anand's population, laid the blame for their plight at various doors.

An attempt was made to ascertain the ability of the respondents to discriminate between government policies on the one hand, and the ministers and bureaucrats who implemented them on the other. People belonging to the young and old generations, who had either recently entered the labour force or were about to quit it, apportioned equal blame to government policies and to the bureaucrats who implemented them. Only the middle generation made a clear distinction between the two and was inclined to hold the latter rather than the former much more responsible. In the generational difference of perspective as to who or what was responsible for the hardship people were experiencing, there was one exception: the Patidars. Having been deeply involved in improving their economic standing in the shortest possible time, largely by means of private enterprise, the Patidars, whatever their age-group, were almost unanimous in blaming government policies for the hardships suffered by the average man.

Subsequently, when the list of those who could possibly be blamed for the hardship was expanded to include black marketeers, businessmen and politicians, a large number of voters apportioned blame in the following order: black marketeers, government policies, bureaucrats, businessmen and, finally, the politicians.

Four years later, in 1971, when there was chaos in state politics as a result of mass defections and the rise and fall of short-lived coalitions, there was a dramatic reversal in the pecking order. Politicians, who had been at the tail-end of the list, moved to the front position. The black marketeers, *vis-à-vis* the defecting or wily politicians, were given some credit for at least exerting themselves a little. The defecting politicians, their critics maintained, did nothing: they merely transferred their political support from one party to another in return for cash or office. Behind such a change lay the integration of generational perspectives on political accountability. No matter where one stood in terms of years, a defectionist politician was reprehensible to all generations.

During the election of 1975 voters in all the age-groups were of the opinion that there was something seriously wrong with government policies. Why, for instance, should the price of edible oil go up before an election, especially in a year when there had been a bumper crop of groundnuts? It was also maintained that the government allowed the millers to charge high prices in return for huge donations to the election funds. While the middle and old generation emphasised the need for public accountability the young generation also underlined the need to mobilise public opinion and protest against such devious practices.

The views of these two generations were also significant in relation to the Navnirman Movement and the declaration of the state of emergency.

The initial reaction of the middle and old generation to the Navnirman Movement was one of fear and dismay. While they were most critical of the policies of the Congress Party in Gujarat and of corruption in high places, they did not altogether welcome the idea of the youth of the country getting involved in the movement at the cost of their attendance in schools and colleges. In the opinion of the middle-aged and the old, the malaise had gone much too deep to be cured by the students' agitations. Even if the present batch of politicians were to be replaced by others, they too, after some time, would resort to corrupt means. This group did however, give credit to the young for making the people deeply aware of the political problem and the need to do something about it.

To the overwhelming majority of young generation voters, the Navnirman Movement was a great event. The bulk of them maintained that it woke up the whole nation and reminded it of the need to punish corrupt politicians. A segment among them felt that the movement could have done much more if only it had been properly organised.

As far as the attitude to the state of emergency was concerned, its most outspoken critics came from among the older men and the educated young. The articulate among the older men spoke of the *misa raj* (government by arbitrary rules under the Maintenance of Internal Security Act – MISA) as the worst kind of *Raj* they had known. Some said Nehru would not have done what his daughter did to her own erstwhile colleagues. That Mahatma Gandhi made people fearless whereas this other Gandhi brought back the fear of government. The educated among them described the emergency as the negation of what was achieved in 1947.

The criticism of the young generation was much more bookish and personalised. Most of them ended their argument by saying that the state of emergency had been declared so that Sanjay Gandhi could be safely installed as a successor to Mrs Gandhi.

Within the middle-aged group a number of people defended the emergency on the ground that it introduced a much-needed discipline, stopped strikes, brought down prices and promised land and housing to the poor. But even they objected to the arbitrary arrests and the general atmosphere of fear it created.

The generational analysis in this chapter will have helped us to identify the specific political characteristics of the people who came of electoral age at different times in the social and historical process of free India. Unlike most other developing countries, the period of India's freedom struggle, as a result of the crystallisation of certain political values and social directions during the period, became an integral part of her socio-political system after independence. The perspectives of the different generations on this organic link, however, remained different. And not to be able to identify the generational perspectives and concerns is to miss the vital periods of destabilisation which marked off one generation from another.

4 Economic Self-perception and Political Response

For students of social sciences one of the greatest puzzles of our time is the absence of revolution or the emergence of class conflict leading to a potentially revolutionary situation in India. In his learned work, *Social Origins of Dictatorship and Democracy* (1966), Barrington Moore, Jr, gave incisive expression to the puzzle:

> Although the Indian peasants have undergone as much material suffering as the Chinese over the last two centuries, India has not yet experienced a peasant revolution. Some possible reasons are already evident from differences in their social structure prior to the western intrusion, as well as from significant variations in the timing and character of that impact. Violence has been a part of the response, though, so far, only as a very minor component. To explain why there has not been a great deal more, it will be necessary to discuss the character of the Indian nationalist movement and the violence that has sporadically erupted.[1]

Moore thus identified the two major factors – the social structure and the nature of the nationalist movement – which together, in his opinion, prevented Indian society from resorting to violent revolution in order to restructure itself. In his book, and particularly in the section on India, Moore described at length the absence of a revolutionary impulse despite great poverty and exploitation of the Indian peasantry. He found such a phenomenon contradicting his own model and was honest enough to admit it. What he did not get down to, however, was a causal analysis of the structural and normative factors underlying the Indian socio-political system which have so far effectively prevented the masses from considering violent revolution as a possible alternative.

In this chapter I shall argue that despite the institutional facilities for the expression of basic demands, as introduced by the new political system,[2] social groups in India have not yet emerged as social classes making economic demands of their own across the traditional divide; and that such groups remain, by and large, pre-class or classless in their economic expectations, political involvement and demand for legislative response. Furthermore, when the formal legislation on the statute book fails to provide the promised results, the traditional social groups remain incapable of generating effective political pressure to secure them.

Since the traditional social groups or castes fail to acquire the characteristics of class, either in their self-perceived economic injustice or in their antagonism to one another, or indeed in their pursuit of remedial political partisanship, the Marxian concept of class does not help very much in conceptual analysis of the Indian puzzle.

Moreover, the main thrust for social change in India since independence has come from political organisations such as the Congress Party and an elite that was committed to social reconstruction rather than in response to the pressure generated by the poor and the exploited. So far as the economically poor and the very poor are concerned, as has already been said, they have initially used their new political status as voters to fight the humiliations of social hierarchy rather than the oppression of poverty.

Finally, in sequential terms, participation ideology in India, with special significance for her hierarchical social structure, preceded the ideology of distributive justice. The institution of universal adult suffrage was nearly a quarter of a century old when the political leadership made an explicit promise at the beginning of this decade to eliminate poverty. Such a sequence had its own far-reaching effect. For one thing it engendered confidence in the openness of the new political system and sustained hope for its possible equitable use in the future. The new political system helped in nibbling away at many of the status-oriented privileges with their roots in the hierarchical social structure. It also laid the foundation for a further assault on the new economic and political power of a non-traditional variety which has concentrated in fewer hands since independence. Such an assault, as we shall presently see, is directed more against the men in office who permit the abuse of public authority to the rich and the powerful rather than at the economic and political arrangements of society in general.

In 1974-5 India experienced mass agitations on an unprecedented scale in certain urban centres, which severely attacked the

inordinate rise in the cost of food, corruption and maladministration in general. For the first time, pressure was put on the
governments of the states and the centre to solve the basic economic
problems. The result was the suspension of civil liberties and the
right to criticise the governments under the Emergency. It was
significant that the democratically enfranchised Indians took three
decades to demand relief from basic economic problems such as the
high cost of food. Moreover, the agitation for relief was confined to
the urban centres of a few states in India.

The chapter will discuss the controversy surrounding the Marxian concept of class and then focus on two aspects of the Indian
experience: the sequential emphasis on the removal first, of the
humiliations of the social hierarchy, and then of the oppression of
poverty; and economic self-perception and voting.

I   THE CONTROVERSY SURROUNDING THE
MARXIAN CONCEPT OF CLASS

One of the most ironical situations in the history of social and
political movements aiming at revolutionary change in the societies
and politics of Europe and North America, is the incomplete and
unsatisfactory state in which Marx left his concept of *class*, which
subsequently became, despite this shortcoming, the central driving
force of those movements. In his writings, Marx used the concept of
class both as a tool of analysis of socio-economic history, and as a
focal-point to which the revolutionary movements could address
themselves. On his part, however, Marx went on postponing the
systematic treatment of this most cherished concept to his mature
years, until suddenly 'death took the pen from his hand'.[3] In the
third volume of his *Das Capital*, the chapter entitled 'The Classes',
which hardly runs into a few lines, there is a comment by his editor,
Frederick Engels, which says: 'here the manuscript breaks off'.[4]
Since then a number of scholars have tried to piece together Marx's
scattered references to the concept of class. One of the boldest
attempts in that direction is Dahrendorf's *Class and Class Conflicts in
Industrial Society*, which did not lose sight of the central question in
Marx, namely that of how societies change. In Dahrendorf's words,
to Marx the theory of class

    was not a theory of a cross section of society arrested in time, in particular not a theory of social stratification, but a tool for the exploitation of changes in total societies. In elaborating and applying his theory of class, Marx was not guided by the question 'how does a given society in fact look at a given point of time' but by the question 'how does the structure of society change?' or, in his own words, 'what is the (economic) law of motion of modern society?'[5]

To Marx, social change was a function of the socio-historical emergence of the *classes* within the productive relationships, in which one of the partners was deeply aware of the economic injustice being done to it, and was seeking to redress this by means of its own consolidation and a political organisation to wage a struggle on its behalf. Bendix and Lipset in their incisive paper 'Karl Marx's Theory of Social Classes' identified the following conditions for class emergence and consequent social change:

> Conflicts over economic rewards; communication between people in the same class-position facilitating the sharing of ideas and action-programmes; the growth of class-consciousness indicating a feeling of solidarity and the understanding of an historic role; the dissatisfaction of the lower class over its inability to control the reward structure; and, the establishment of a political organization with the explicit purpose of fundamentally altering the basic productive relations.[6]

The Marxian approach to the emergence of the social classes did not extend to peasant societies because of certain inherent difficulties. From the point of view of Marx what characterises a peasant society is the fact of *isolation* among people occupying similar class positions within the productive relationships.[7] Unlike the working class, the people in peasant societies neither develop a sense of common identity nor enter into what Marx described as 'manifold relations with one another',[8] one of which can be political, leading to the establishment of a political organisation to fight for their common economic interests. Such an isolation is further reinforced by the vertical barriers of the social organisation and the horizontal divides of the village system. So far as Indian society was concerned, Marx had hoped that British rule would play the historical role of sweeping away the divisiveness of the 'village communities', transforming it into some sort of a bourgeois society; from then on social change in India would fall into the same pattern as he had envisaged for the industrial societies of the West.

Max Weber questioned Marx's emphasis on the working class as conscious of his historical role in social transformation, and as engaging in substantive conflict through the medium of a political organisation. Apart from the fact that to Weber the concept of class was not always an effective tool of analysis for all stages of social and historical process, the incidence of 'genuine class struggles' in Europe was far more limited than Marx had envisaged.[9] What had characterised all kinds of social systems, according to Weber, was the struggle between their status groups.

In questioning Marx, Dahrendorf went a step further than Max Weber. To contemporary industrial society, to which Dahrendorf gave the name 'post-capitalist', the following two statements by Marx had little relevance: 'Individuals form class only in so far as they are engaged in a common struggle with another class;'[10] and ' . . . Organization of the proletariat as a class, and that means as a political party, eventually furnishes the basis of class struggle. To repeat, every class struggle is a political struggle.'[11]

According to Dahrendorf, what Marx was suggesting here was that class conflict results in a political party which ultimately pursues organisational action for its aim of social transformation. To Dahrendorf such a performance on the part of the working class in the industrial societies of the West of today was inconceivable for two reasons. First, the unity and homogeneity of the working class, which Marx idealised, does not exist in any society. The composition of the labour force, pursuing diverse occupations, has drastically changed, and is enough to make any concerted action on the part of the working class an impossibility. Second, the mobility and drive towards equality have 'steered class structures and conflicts in directions unforeseen by Marx'.[12]

Tom Bottomore, a Marxist of the finest intellectual tradition of Europe, supporting Dahrendorf's conclusions, maintained that, 'the coincidence of economic conflict and political conflict', which is at the root of Marxian theory of class, has ceased to exist in post-capitalist society.[13]

The upshot of the above controversy surrounding the concept of class is two-fold: first, the kind of class conflict issuing in a political organisation to wage a struggle on behalf of the deprived class, about which Marx spoke, does not correspond with the realities of the collective bargaining which goes on in industrial societies of our time; and, second, Marx himself did not extend his class analysis or the feasibility of any political action based on it to the traditional agricultural societies. Moreover, colonial rule, particularly in India, instead of sweeping away the horizontal and vertical social structures of the traditional societies left them more or less untouched. The main thrust of the colonial powers remained largely confined to the areas of revenue and judicial administration. What colonial rule failed to achieve directly, however, was gradually being achieved by democratic ideology and political institutions which were boldly transplanted by the indigenous elite *after* the colonial era had ended. There is now sufficient evidence that democratic institutions have struck root in India. Any discussion on social change must, therefore, take this into account as a central fact.

II THE THRUST TOWARDS THE REMOVAL OF SOCIAL HIERARCHY AND POVERTY

As noted earlier, Max Weber made a significant distinction between caste and ethnicity. For him, in a society with ethnic plurality, the question of 'honour' was relative to specific ethnic groups.[14] In a society based on caste, on the other hand, the dimension of hierarchy is added on the question of honour. What is more, throughout the recorded span of Indian history, the Hindu social organisation, with its spokesmen confined to the higher strata, regarded social hierarchy as a desirable norm. This has left behind deep scars of humiliation on the middle as well as the lower strata of Hindu society. It has also created many obstacles to concerted action within the social organisation as a whole. A three-decade-old Indian democratic republic and a number of intensely contested elections have socialised the Indians into a common political citizenship across the traditional social divisions. A commensurable development in the economic field, whereby the individual would claim and be assured of his minimum economic rights, and an effective political organisation to back him up, has yet to take place. Any theoretical explanation of the way in which the average Indian looks forward to the solution of his economic problems at the hands of the men he has elected to various levels of authority must take into account the following three dimensions of the situation which condition his expectations and behaviour. They are:

(a) the interaction between the traditional social organisation and the new political system;
(b) the ideological commitment of the political elite;
(c) contradictions in the performance of the political system and its failure to produce the promised results.

We shall now examine each of these in some detail.

TRADITIONAL SOCIAL ORGANISATION AND THE NEW POLITICAL SYSTEM

The social organisation confronted by the new political system has shown a greater propensity towards loosening up the traditional relationships in political rather than in economic matters. That is to say that over the years there has been an effective response from the various castes towards the diversification of their electoral choices and thereby the building up of multi-caste support for political organisations, rather than in the formation of effective economic bases across the ascriptive boundaries for the pursuit of common economic goals. Once we move away from urban centres and their unionised labour in specific industries, only party organisations, in a vague and often misleading fashion, claim to represent the economic demands of the wage-earners.

In Anand, a rapidly industrialising middle-sized city, where some of these ideas were empirically tested, the segment of unionised labour, despite increase in union membership in recent years, was not very significant. With a population of about 100,000, Anand has fourteen medium scale industries and Asia's largest and most prestigious milk co-operative dairy, AMUL. Its unionised labour was mainly confined to industrial, transport, municipal, insurance, banking and educational enterprises. The sharp rise in the cost of living in recent years also stimulated the increase in union membership. It rose from 6 per cent in 1967 to about 25 per cent in 1975 in the types of enterprise mentioned. The bulk of the labour force, however, did not enjoy the same protection.

So far as the interaction between social organisation and the new political system is concerned the most significant thing to note is the change in the character of the social groups and in their inter-group relationships as each was inducted into the democratic process.

Elsewhere we have identified this in detail.[15] Sequentially speaking,
the democratic process in India first of all became an instrument for
questioning the hierarchy at the root of the country's social
organisation, then, in a limited way, together with the support
received from the ideological commitments of a political elite, of the
appalling economic injustice and poverty. Initially, therefore, the
democratic process became an instrument of caste rather than class
antagonism. Practically all over India, with the introduction of the
new political system power shifted from the upper castes to the
numerically more powerful middle-caste agriculturists. They, as
well as the lower castes as an auxiliary political force, used their new
political status to generate a drive towards higher social recognition.
In private conversations with research investigators their in-
dications of social self-ranking were way out of line with what was
commonly acknowledged. The first wave of their assault was
directed towards the regaining of their 'honour', to use Max
Weber's term. Out of the four major castes of Anand – those of the
Brahmins, Banias, Patidars and Kshatriyas (the last two of them
agriculturist castes) – the Patidars were an exception. Unlike their
predecessors of half a century ago, who made use of the census as
well as the genealogist to register higher social origin, the Patidars of
the 1960s, economically prosperous and politically well-
entrenched, did not worry about their 'honour' *vis-à-vis* the other
castes. Instead, together with the Brahmins and the Banias, all
upper or upper-middle castes, they concentrated on economic
problems. From the Kashatriyas downwards, however, the question
of relative 'honour' remained paramount. Without wishing for the
disappearance of the traditional social structure, what they were
hoping to do, through the instrumentality of the new political
status, was to horizontalise an essentially vertical structure and
thereby eliminate the question of social subordination and super-
ordination between them and their traditional superiors. The first
wave of their assault, then, had left in the background the more
fundamental question of economic justice to the poor. Vaguely they
looked to the government to help the poor by means of legislative
and bureaucratic protection. Furthermore, they continued to couch
the economic responsibilities of the government in traditional and
moral terms.

As we have already seen, the election of 1962, which had
proliferated the diversification of votes among all the major social
and religious groups, also registered an increased understanding on

the part of the voters regarding the use of political alternatives to resolve their economic problem. This meant that they started reviewing the administrative and economic performance of the party in power in terms of how it affected their day-to-day life and related this to their own electoral decision-making. Such a process was accelerated by the increased volume of cynical floor-crossing between 1967 and 1971 on the one hand, and Mrs Gandhi's slogan of *garibi hatao* (eradicate poverty) on the other.

THE IDEOLOGICAL COMMITMENT OF THE POLITICAL ELITE

In raising the question of the economic responsibility of government machinery, and more particularly economic growth with distributive justice, the constitution of the Indian republic, the Congress Party ideology and the commitment of a generation of elite and their agitations in urban centres, played a more vital role than the organised demand from the poor strata of Indian society. Unlike the social historical change envisaged by the Marxian theory of class, where class-consciousness has its consequences in the formation of political organisations to serve class interests, economic factor preceding political factor, the Indian situation for nearly three decades following independence has been the other way around. The decision to give new political status to the masses by means of universal adult suffrage, and the official policy of the Congress Party of working towards a casteless and classless society, were essentially political decisions inspired by the ideological commitments of the generation of political elite which led the nationalist movement and also governed the country after independence. Such decisions were not taken by way of concessions to class demands. Nehru and other notable leaders would have remained in office till the end of their lives even if they had not introduced political democracy and the official ideology of socialism. There was no class compulsion on them to do so. In the final analysis it was their moral choices working themselves out in political decisions, undictated by class considerations, but largely arrived at by their own understanding of soicety and the norms of social justice.

While the initial thrust towards social change in the post-independence period came from the top political leadership, two decades later it transformed itself into a popular demand. Instead of the earlier emphasis on reconstructing society by way of public participation, economic development *through* distributive justice was brought into the centre of public debate. Political decisions relating to secularism, democracy and socialism have helped in engendering a view of government as an instrument of change and in converting economic difficulties into economic demands. Three decades of political socialisation of the new political system have helped in preparing the masses to view its performance in economic terms. Consequently, when Mrs Gandhi, campaigning for the election of 1971, adopted the crucial slogan *garibi hatao*, it at once crystallised the groping public attitude to the economic responsibility of government machinery. The irradication of poverty slogan thus had administrative rather than class connotations.

The average man, distressed by his worsening economic condition, had stopped couching the economic responsibility of the government in moral terms as he had done in the past. Instead he now looked at his hardships as a problem for the administrators to solve.

CONTRADICTIONS IN THE POLITICAL SYSTEM AND ITS FAILURE TO ACHIEVE RESULTS

Each professedly socialist measure introduced since independence, owing to the inherent contradictions in the socio-historical process of contemporary India, has produced non-egalitarian results. The backlog of problems, the pro-vested interest attitude of bureaucracy and the middle-level political workers, as well as the failure of the masses effectively to back up their demands, have together produced non-socialist results at each stage. The socialist promises of the Congress Party thus far, have outstretched its capacity to fulfil them. Consequently, each professedly socialist measure produced more disparities and more tensions. Somewhere down the line the benefits intended for the average man did not reach him. Western social science, which universally provides theoretical perspectives and tools of analysis, has sensitised scholars either to look to the bureaucratic and political upper echelons, or to the grass-roots base, or to explain situations exclusively in terms of one *or* the other. Speaking of the problem of legislation implementation, what is most baffling is the middle rung of the political and bureaucratic hierarchy which, since Indian independence, has successfully thwarted the pursuit of intended goals. The study of this middle rung has not so far received adequate attention.

The contradiction between the professed goals of the policy-makers and the results they achieve are viewed by the average voter in semi-class terms. He tends to group together the ministers, the officials and their *sagawalas* (relatives), the rich, and the influential – who get the most out of the system – into one broad category, the *mota, mota loko* (the big and influential people), as against another group, namely, that of the poor. His essential evaluation of the *mota, mota loko* is done not in terms of productive relationships, but as the usurpers of public authority for private gain. What is significant here is the fact that the economic groupings are designated with reference to the political system and public authority rather than to the productive relationships of which Marx spoke. Consequently, the conflict between the two groups becomes a political conflict for producing the desired economic results. In such a conflict the rich are seen not as having their *own* government, but as usurping the duly constituted public authority with the connivance of the elected deputies. It is the overall consequences of policy implementation that remain at the centre of voter attention, not the class-conflicts. For the average voter it is the elected deputies who join in or permit the public exploitation who are at fault, rather than the bourgeoisie as such. The latter is no doubt held to be a corrupting influence, but the failure to discharge responsibility by the politician remains the main target of criticism. In the final analysis the frame-work of criticism continues to be in political terms for economic goals.

The events of 1974–7, involving protests against the heavy rise in the cost of living and corruption in high places, the imposition of the Emergency, and the curtailment of civil liberties, have all made the people much more aware of the need to implement public policy in the common interest, and of how to make their own demands towards that aim more effective.

III   ECONOMIC SELF-PERCEPTION AND VOTING

'Have you prospered, declined or remained where you were in the Congress Raj?'

An attempt was made to elicit a reply to this direct question. Couched in the simplest possible economic terms, its aim was to establish whether, under the democratic political system as man-aged by the Congress Party for three decades, the respondents had prospered, declined, or remained where they were.

The response was then analysed from three points of view: (i) in units of social organisation; (ii) in occupational categories within the economy; and (iii) with reference to income. The object of the exercise was not merely to obtain a straightforward correlation between units of society or economy, economic self-evaluation and vote, but to examine the variety of explanations which emerged around the question itself and how they became critical to the shaping of the vote.

In a number of cases the answers relating to economic self-evaluation were nothing but a rationalisation and preparation for the vote. At times certain respondents had stated that although they had prospered in the Congress *Raj*, they did not intend to vote for the party. A possible implication of this was that they gave themselves the entire credit for their prosperity. Conversely, the intention to vote for the Congress Party in the absence of economic prosperity indicated the hope of better days to come under the Congress *Raj*. But in 1975, a striking shift from this position was in evidence. Those who had felt that they were worse off in the Congress *Raj*, began to explore, in large numbers, a political alternative to it.

SOCIAL GROUPS AND THE ECONOMIC RATIONALE FOR VOTING

The economic rationale for voting in any society, developed or developing, is far more complex than can be deduced from examining who gained what from a certain set of party policies. As we have just seen, not all the communities who claimed to have prospered during the Congress *Raj*, gave commensurate electoral support to the party. With the exception of the Kshatriyas and Muslims, the general tendency on the part of the groups was to favour the ruling party with less support than their claim to prosperity warranted.

Moreover, different social and religious groups put forward different degrees of economic argument before making their electoral decisions. At times the economic rationale put forward by the same group for party support differed from election to election, and in some cases they even radically altered their retrospective assessments. In a short span its perspectives changed and its assessment of its own past performance changed with it.

Never in any single social group did the economic argument become a necessary and sufficient condition for giving its vote to the Congress Party in all three elections. In certain cases it did for up to two elections, then other factors prevailed.

The Patidars as well as the Kshatriyas could, at one point in time, relate their economic well-being to two different economic philosophies: the large measure of uninhibited economic activity proposed by the Swantantra Party, and the rigid control over the economy with some measure of distributive justice, proposed by the Congress Party. But the only election which presented such well-defined alternatives, at least in Gujarat, was that of 1967. It had for the first time provided scope for voting on the basis of a clear-cut economic argument. The two subsequent elections, however, raised issues and slogans which made the contesting parties merely omnibus vote-catchers.

The electoral support for the Congress Party in the three upper castes of Brahmins, Banias and Patidars was not commensurate with the prosperity that they had claimed under its *Raj*. Their relatively greater diversity of occupation, together with the independent and semi-independent nature of such occupations, had made them give more credit to themselves for their prosperity. In contrast, the Kshatriyas' support for the Congress Party, being largely a wage-earning and therefore economically dependent class, far outweighed the little prosperity that came their way under its *Raj*. Finally, the Christians and Muslims, having been preoccupied with the secular future of Indian society, were just about beginning to turn their attention to the economic question and vote.

The most striking development, however, appeared during the election of 1975, when there was a strong correlation between the negative economic evaluation of the Congress Party and the votes of the Brahmins, Banias and Patidars, and to some extent those of the Kshatriyas, Christians and Muslims. The economic dimension of voting in Anand had at last begun to crystallise as it manifested itself in this negative correlation.

OCCUPATIONAL RATIONALE AND ELECTORAL RESPONSE

This brings us to the related question of occupational rationale and vote. One's economic self-assessment essentially takes place within the framework of the occupation that one pursues. The percentage of Brahmins, Banias, Patidars, Kshatriyas, Christians and Muslims in our sample fell into the following occupational categories:

	%
housewives	46
businessmen	21
cultivators	7
employees	26

(a) Housewives

During the elections of 1967, 1971, 1972 and 1975, the electoral responses of housewives registered a series of changes, doubtless reflecting the influence of their husbands and children of voting age, the anguish and reaction to the continued rise in the cost of living and their attraction to the personality of Mrs Gandhi as a woman leader, especially after 1971. Their support for the Congress Party was as follows: 1967 (45 per cent); 1971 (35 per cent); 1972 (54 per cent); and 1975 (57 per cent).

Between the elections of 1967 and 1971, the support of the housewives for the Congress Party dwindled considerably. The greatest single factor responsible for this was the phenomenal rise in the cost of living, the difficulties experienced in obtaining various food items and articles of daily use, and above all the skilful exploitation of such difficulties by the rival political organisations. Women visited the grocery stores and vegetable markets as many times as men did. The rocketing price structure of some foods, together with the continual decline in the purchasing power of their hard-earned rupee, was a personal experience for all of them. Consequently, when Mrs Gandhi came out, in 1971, with her slogan of eradicating poverty, the housewives were naturally sceptical, probably more than their husbands.

During the election of 1975, the Congress vote among the housewives registered a slight increase. While the bulk of the housewives from Brahmin, Bania, Patidar and Christian communities showed a marked preference for the Janata, the rest did not. Despite the fact that Kshatriya and Muslim housewives, too, were extremely critical of corruption and the cost of living under the Congress regime, only a small percentage among them joined the other housewives in search of political alternative to the party. In this respect the Kshatriya and Muslim housewives proved even more passive than their menfolk. Being more sheltered than the other womenfolk, it was more difficult for them to break the long tradition of voting for the Congress Party.

(b) Businessmen

The businessmen of Anand – the bulk of them Brahmins, Banias and Patidars – bitterly complained about the hostile attitude and policies of the Congress Party towards the business community in general. The various regulations governing economic activity, to their way of thinking merely stifled economic development and provided an opportunity for corrupt bureaucrats and politicians to make money at their expense. Nor were they happy with the tax burden imposed on them by the Congress government. Over the years the variations in their support for the party were as follows: 1967 (47 per cent); 1971 (22 per cent); 1972 (39 per cent); and 1975 (50 per cent).

During the election of 1967, despite their great attraction to the ideology and programme of the Swatantra Party, few of the businessmen were bold enough to support the opposition party in a big way. Most of them were convinced of the Congress Party's victory and therefore did not want to alienate it. In 1971, with the Organisation Congress in power in Gujarat, the businessmen took a courageous step in defying the Ruling Congress, which was still groping for a political base in the state. Finally, in the following year the need for political stability in the state and the realisation that the bark of the Ruling Congress was worse than its bite, persuaded some businessmen to return to its fold. A quarter of a century of socialistic professions and policy formulations, but highly questionable implementation, on the part of the Congress Party had taught the businessmen not to get too unduly upset. Its slogans and policies were one thing, but their implementation was an altogether different matter. Regardless of the political philosophy currently in vogue in New Delhi, the administrative machinery could be induced to serve the interests of the businessmen. Cynically, some of the articulate businessmen maintained that they very much welcomed the Congress Party's brand of socialism.

(c) Cultivators

The cultivators of Anand largely consisted of Patidars and Kshatriyas. While the former owned more land, the latter predominated numerically. By its failure to produce the promised changes in the land-tenure system by means of the Land Tenancy Act, the

Congress Party had succeeded in attracting the landless Kshatriyas and repelling the land-owning Patidars. The following almost unchanging vote for the Congress Party, over the years, reflected the continued Kshatriyas support: 1967 (55 per cent); 1971 (50 per cent); 1972 (51 per cent); and 1975 (85 per cent).

During the election of 1975, there was a swing in the cultivators' vote for the Congress Party, especially among those who were resident in Anand. These cultivators were either Kshatriya small-scale land-owners or Patidars with large pieces of cultivable land. The former had pinned all their hopes on the Congress Party, and the latter had benefited greatly by cash crops of tobacco and cotton. For all its formal threats concerning the implementation of the land-tenure policy the Congress Party had done precious little in actual practice. Consequently, the big landowners resident in Anand were immensely pleased with the Congress Party.

(d) Employees
In terms of its caste composition, this category of occupation was a highly mixed group. It encompassed people who were employed in government, municipality and public and private concerns. Economically speaking, it consisted of a lower-middle and wage-earning class. Like the housewives, another socially heterogeneous group, the electoral response of the employees was governed by the cost of living. Over the years, its support for the Congress Party reflected its hope, frustration and resurgent hope, and another round of disillusionment: 1967 (48 per cent); 1971 (38 per cent); 1972 (51 per cent); and 1975 (38 per cent).

The employees earned fixed incomes which were perpetually out of line with the soaring cost of living. The competition for jobs resulting from unemployment, together with the limited un-ionisation of labour, put the employees in a poor bargain capacity *vis-à-vis* their employers. Their only hope was government in-tervention, especially in fixing up a fair wage, defining conditions of service and above all arresting the price rises. Initially sceptical of Mrs Gandhi's slogan of eradicating poverty, like the housewives the employees, too, turned to the Ruling Congress in 1972 with renewed hopes.

But during the election of 1975, the Congress Party received a hard knock at the hands of the employees. Nearly four years had passed since Mrs Gandhi had announced her slogan of eradication of poverty. Instead of that the average person on a fixed income had to experience a great deal of hardship and a decline in his standard of living.

Before we conclude this chapter it may be worth while to have a look at the related question of income and voting behaviour. In order to analyse this relationship we divided our respondents into three income groups, as follows:

(a) those who earned less than Rs 300 per month: the lower income group;
(b) those who earned above Rs 300 and below Rs 1200 per month: the middle income group;
(c) those who earned above Rs 1200 per month: the upper income group.

In the low income group, support for the Congress Party was broad-based. With the exception of the Banias, the support for the Party in this income group was fairly widespread. This was a group without much initiative of its own which looked to government agencies and private firms for employment and economic advancement. Since most of them lacked education and skills, they seemed to blame themselves rather than the Congress Party.

In the middle income group, with the exception of the Kshatriyas and Muslims, the Congress Party did not enjoy much support. This group consisted of skilled workers, businessmen and office workers. Their education and skills had roused their expectations of a higher standard of living than they in fact enjoyed. This was also the group which complained bitterly against the rising cost of essential commodities and the continual threat to its standard of living.

Finally, the people in the upper income group consisted of the Banias and Patidars who ran the flourishing business houses of Anand. Over the years they had learned to manipulate the so-called socialist policies of the Congress Party to their own advantage. Consequently, the majority of them were not keen on an alternative. In 1975, the Congress Party, enjoyed the following volume of support: low income group (70 per cent); middle income group (39 per cent); and, upper income group (57 per cent).

To conclude, in this chapter we have examined the inadequacy of the class model to explain the source, idiom and direction of social change in contemporary India. In the post-independence period particularly, the initiative for a radical change had come not so much from the economically poor section of the society as from a generation of political elite, comprising the upper middle-class, which was ideologically committed to the eradication of social hierarchy and poverty. Such an elite mainly worked through the Congress Party and on its periphery. With the exception of a few specific areas, its efforts had been counter-productive. This was mainly due to two reasons. First, it narrowly defined its own role as one of influencing public policy rather than obtaining tangible results therefrom. It thus ended up by subscribing to the statute-book socialism of the Congress Party. In so doing it merely pursued what I would like to call the politics of good conscience. Second, while, as a political organisation, the Congress Party held itself increasingly accountable for the economic results of its policies, the effective political pressure on it to achieve the results it had promised could not be generated from below until the middle of the 1970s. In the meantime the socialistically inclined elite preferred to act as consultants to the Congress Party rather than to organise the poor and force the party to implement its policies effectively. The average voter, left to himself, with no pro-poor viable political alternative to the Congress Party, in the successive elections merely played the game of give and not give votes to the Party for three decades.

We also noticed in this chapter at the level of the individual the new political status resulting from his enfranchisement under universal suffrage, was used by him first of all against the social hierarchy then, marginally, against poverty. Only when the doors to social mobility in areas other than the age-old stratified endogamous groups opened up, did the bulk of the voters turn their attention towards the instrumental use of their new political status to fight poverty. In the early phase of their enfranchisement, in other words, the performance of the Congress Party in solving economic difficulties received only a part of the newly enfranchised voters' attention. What forced the voters to pay greater attention to the results of the Congress Party's policies was their ever-worsening economic plight. There again, as we saw in the foregoing pages, it was not the poor (Kshatriyas) but the relatively better off (the Patidars) who actively went in search of a political alternative to the Congress Party. So far as the poor and the very poor were concerned, initially they remained far more preoccupied with their place in the social hierarchy than with the solution of their economic problems. Their emphasis on economic problems began to increase as their new political status as voters assured them of growing equality within the hierarchical social order itself.

In a sense the mass agitation, which was spearheaded by the youth of Gujarat and Bihar in 1974–5 against economic hardship as a result of corruption and maladministration, acted as a catalyst. It brought to the centre of everybody's attention the need to put pressure on those who made public policy and implemented it. From then on, other considerations receded into the background even among those who until recently had been obsessed with the question of social honour. The phenomenon of mass agitation for relief from economic hardships also opened up the scope for concerted action across the traditional divide. Since below a certain income level a common awareness of hardships could no longer be segmented even by the traditional divisions, the need to do something *together* about it, by all those who were in a similar situation, began to be discussed in more and more groups. At that stage a potential participation in agitation on the part of the poor became a distinct possibility. Initially it reflected itself in the form of interest and sympathy for the goal of the youthful agitators followed by a merciless denunciation of those in power, their relatives and commercial interests in general. But before such a process could fully crystallise itself into an effective force which could not be further misled by empty promises, the imposition of the state of emergency created the need for another kind of priority – the restoration of the mechanisms and institutions of participation.

Between the years 1974–7, a massive dose of populism was injected into the Indian political society. From the mass agitation preceding the Emergency to the widespread discussion of the right of recall as implicit in democracy in the post-1977 election period, what had been underlined was the performance, accountability and probationary character of those in power. Against such a background, the growing identity of the poor was likely to result in the exploration of a range of possible political action, unprecedented in democratic India.

5 Party Organisation, Campaigning and Voter Contact

In various scholarly writings on party organisation, relating to Western as well as Indian democracy, a number of models have been proposed to interpret the social bases and functions of political parties in those societies. Most of these models tend to treat political parties as formal political structures prescribing a number of specific roles to their members. In this chapter, however, I shall argue that such an emphasis tends to leave out a whole range of operative relationships between the members of competing political parties on the one hand, and of party members and the public on the other. Such relationships fall outside the formal role-definition of the members. These relationships, nevertheless, become of paramount importance in understanding party organisations in India, where members do not don the party uniform all the time but tend to return to their normal social ties in between elections, and in most cases alternate between party strife and inter-party accommodation.

The discussion in this chapter is divided into three broad categories. The first will examine the various models, including my own, which aim at understanding the roles and functions of party organisations. The second and third sections will examine the changing nature of electoral campaigning and voter contact in Anand.

I MODELS FOR PARTY ORGANISATION

THE CLEAVAGE MODEL

One of the classic expositions of this model is Robert Alford's *Party and Society: The Anglo-American Democracies* (1964). In this work

Alford claimed that he was testing the hypothesis provided by *Voting*, by Berelson *et al*, that 'voting cleavages' could be traced back to class, ethnicity and ecological divisions in the population. From voting statistics, mainly in Great Britain, Australia, the USA and Canada, Alford inferred that in those countries, especially in the early 1960s, there was a strong evidence of class voting. Among the four countries mentioned, Britain, according to him, was much more class-oriented in voting than the rest. From this premise Alford reached the conclusion that their political parties, too, were based on the cleavages of class.[1]

Simultaneously, S. M. Lipset in *The Political Man: The Social Bases of Politics*, also undertook a class analysis of political parties in Western democracies. Lipset reached the conclusion that party strife in those countries was basically a reflection of the class cleavage.[2]

An inconclusive controversy surrounded the view that class was the basis of political cleavage in Britain. Goldthorpe, Lockwood *et al* in *The Affluent Worker* argued that affluence had changed life-styles rather than leading to an instrumental approach to trade unions and politics in general.[3]

Robert MacKenzie and Allan Silver put another point of view. In their *Angel in Marble*, they pointed out that since 1885 nearly one-third of the working class in Britain has been voting for the Tories.[4]

In his subsequent writings, Lipset broadened the definition of the sources of political cleavage so as to include the non-economic factors, and his interest shifted from class to genesis, persistence, interpenetration and the coalitional character of the cleavages that underlie party strife.[5]

Earlier, we examined a parallel model of caste-party identity offered by Srinivas and Harrison to explain the translation of social cleavage into competitive political parties in India. For them the party strife between the Congress and Communist Parties in Andhra state was merely a reflection of the social cleavage between the two peasant castes, the Reddis and Kammas.

The Alford-Lipset and Srinivas-Harrison class and caste models, which attempt to explain the sources of cleavage in political parties, were in the last analysis an over-simplification of the influence of the two vital factors. Neither class nor caste can become the sole basis of the cleavages that underlie party organisations.

THE CONVERSATION-BARGAIN MODEL

Morris-Jones proposed a conversation-bargain model to explain party organisation in India. For him the Congress Party, despite its 'dominance' in the past, stood in a peculiar relationship with those other parties which 'dissented' away from it. He likened the Congress Party to a flabby shopkeeper in an Indian bazaar where 'bargaining and dissent are the language of discourse'.[6] The peculiar relationship between the Congress and the other political parties was made possible by what he called the 'openness' in the former:

> there is a most important 'openness' in the relation between the Congress and the other political parties: not merely is there an absence of barriers, there is a positive communication and interaction between them. The opposition parties neither alternate with Congress in the exercise of power, nor do they share power in any coalition form; rather they operate by *conversing* with sections of Congress itself. They address themselves not so much to the policy-deaf electorate as to like-minded political groups in the dominant party.[7]

A similar conclusion was reached by R. Kothari: 'The role of opposition parties in India is quite distinctive. Instead of providing an alternative to the Congress party, they function by influencing sections within the Congress.'[8]

The election of 1967 and the subsequent political development, did not bear this out however. They showed that the opposition parties were not merely content with the role of influencing certain sections within the Congress Party. They in fact fiercely contested for power, as they would in any other country, and unseated the Congress Party in nearly half the states of India and in the centre. Regardless of the manifold activities in which the opposition parties engaged themselves, their *raison d'être* was the pursuit of power, formal as well as informal.

Nevertheless, by underlining the 'positive communication and interaction' between the Congress Party and the opposition parties, Morris-Jones's conversation-bargain model came pretty close to identifying the realities of the period between the elections. No political party in a democratic society can put a formal cast of hostility on the entire range of socio-political relationships which exist between the members of politically opposing parties. Moreover, the period between elections, in particular, is often conducive to thawing and bargaining, and even allows for making fresh permutations and combinations of people across the party lines. The members of the two rival parties, Congress and Swatantra, as we shall see in this chapter, entered into peculiar alliances and combinations in between elections, in order to transact the business of various institutions.

THE MANIPULATION MODEL

It is impossible to talk about party organisations in any society without referring to their vital function of manipulating popular support for the goals that they set forth. Avery Leiserson in *Parties and Politics* (1958) and Myron Weiner in *Party Building in a New State* (1967) came out with some of the most sophisticated arguments in support of their manipulation models in order to explain the role of party organisation in the developed and developing countries, respectively.

Leiserson accorded to party organisation the function of 'manipulating' the structural relationship between the social system on the one hand, and policy-making mechanisms on the other. From his point of view, party organisations aspire to rise to positions from where they can manipulate or channel the 'conflicting pressures of influential groups' and the official makers of public policy (the bureaucracy) into policy decisions that are acceptable to themselves. The manipulative efforts of party organisations wade through the conflicting interests in society and the rigid behaviour patterns and perspectives of public officials:

> Between the unorganized citizen-voter and the public official, the party organization develops a corporate ideology, a leadership corps, a collective discipline, loyalties, and professional skills which set the party politicians off from both the voters and the permanent government employees.[9]

Weiner explained the uniqueness of the Congress Party – a party which had regularly conducted elections and won them in most cases, worked for political stability, national integration, economic development and which had succeeded in legitimising new and unfamiliar institutions through which social and political conflicts could be resolved – with the help of his manipulation model.

According to him the manipulative operations of the Congress Party were directed towards maintaining itself as an *organisation*; that is, in a politically effective shape. The party also manipulated a close 'fit' between its interests as a party and those of its members. Above everything else, it developed a most effective internal mechanism for manipulating and resolving internal conflicts.
In Weiner's words:

[The Congress] adapts itself to the local power structures. It recruits from among those who have local power and influence. It trains its cadre to perform political roles similar to those performed in the traditional society before there was party politics. It manipulates factional, caste, and linguistic disputes and uses its influence within the administration to win and maintain electoral and financial support. It utilizes traditional methods of dispute settlement to maintain cohesion *within* the party.[10]

Unfortunately, the Weiner model suffered from a discretely dichotomous notion of the role of a party like the Congress on the one hand, and the state on the other. Involved in the manipulation of the social forces, the Congress Party was seen by Weiner as 'adapting' itself to the traditional social reality, whereas the state was characterised as modernistic in its aspirations.

Before and after independence, the Congress Party evolved a number of innovative, rational and secular ideas, perspectives and policy directions which had invariably become guidelines for the party in office. Speaking of Anand and its surroundings, it was the party which had launched the co-operative movement which resulted in the establishment of AMUL. It is equally erroneous to assume that all that the state does is necessarily directed towards modernisation. Through its institutional framework and bureaucracy it consolidates not only the fruits of its own innovations, but also those of the total life of the society and its dynamics.

The adaptive-innovative dichotomy was drawn far too rigidly by Weiner than was necessary for his manipulation model. Despite that, along with Lieserson, he came out with a useful insight into one of the major roles of party organisations, namely that of manipulating the social forces towards party goals.

THE REFLEXIVE MODEL

In his seminal work *Political Parties: A Behavioral Analysis*, Samuel J. Eldersveld adopted a structural-functional approach to explain the character and functions of party organisation in Western democracies. For his analysis he formulated what may be called a reflexive model. That is to say, in his way of thinking, party organisation *reflects* the principal characteristics of society and polity, as it is required to operate between the two. Like the society, it functions as a 'patterned activity' with defined roles for its member actors, boundaries within which to pursue their activities, communication network and goals as subjectively perceived by the members and formally set forth by the organisation. Then, like a polity, the party organisation has its own authority structure, representative process and a mechanism for recruiting new members.[11] A party organisation essentially becomes a 'conflict system' because of the diversity in goal perception, power drives, and factional fights among its members. Added to this are the strains and stresses of continual recruitment at the base, sides and top of the organisation. In the final analysis a party organisation can survive, like the polity, only if it develops an adquate mechanism for resolving those conflicts.

The attempt made by Eldersveld to look at party organisation in terms of a miniaturised analogue of society and polity, was largely through the conceptual framework of structural-functionalism. The critical Parsonian term used by him was 'patterned activity' to describe the gross mass of activity both in society and in party organisation. The underlying assumption, both in the case of Parsons and after him in Eldersveld, was that there is only *one* kind of 'patterned activity', the chief characteristics of which are identifiable. If this is a fair rendering of Eldersveld's approach then it would not be incorrect to say that he had oversimplified the complex range of party organisation activities.

THE STRIFE-ACCOMMODATION MODEL

This brings us to the strife-accommodation model which, in our opinion, explains the sequence of electoral strife alternating with different degrees of inter-party accommodation between elections. We shall examine the interpretive capacity of this model with reference to the field-data on party organisations in Anand.

But before we go on to the examination of the strife-accommodation process in which party organisations are involved, we shall analyse the linkage function which is attributed to them, whereby they link the citizenry with the political system. They bring about such a linkage by aggregating the interests of the citizens and then collectively making a case for looking after them when they come into power.

Party linkage theorists, however, pay too much attention to the interest-aggregation function of party organisation to the exclusion of other less positive forms of linkage. Such theorists also tend to overlook those pursuits of party organisers which do not help either to sustain the existing linkages or to forge new ones. Like all other organisations, the political party has its own inner dynamic, geared to a variety of pursuits. The linkage functions that one reads about in standard works on the subject seem to be drawn from what the party does during elections. What takes the place of such functions between elections? Does the party organisation continue to work towards the persistence of already created linkages at all levels, or does it neglect them or even enter into pursuits which erode them?

In this section I shall argue that we must make a functional distinction between three different kinds of linkage: interest linkages, normative linkages and operational linkages. Of the three I shall concentrate on operational linkages, and I shall argue that the activity of those who run the party organisation during and between elections is substantially different. I will argue further that their activity can be explained with the help of what I would call a strife-accommodation model. This material will be discussed under the following three headings: (a) the three different types of linkage; (b) a model of political party strife-accommodation; and (c) strife-accommodation in Anand.

(a)   The three different types of linkage
As far as interest linkage is concerned, its theorists have supplied us with a number of useful studies.[12] They point out that various structures in society articulate their respective interests and that the party organisation, in order to have their support, formulates programmes balancing the demands of such structures. In so doing the party organisation undertakes a two-fold linkage function: on the one hand it links the competitive demands of different structures to a common programme, and on the other it relates the citizenry to

the political system, by asking it to support the party programme at the polls.

Around such a core activity, the party organisation also becomes the supplier of information and brings together 'unacquainted individuals who share political beliefs, interests, and aspirations'.[13]

Few studies, however, have taken note of what Morton Grodzins calls 'the internal dynamics' of party organisation. In his view party activity is more likely to exacerbate than to aggregate the claims of competing social groups.[14] In fact, as we shall see in this section, between elections party organisations may pursue activities which have very little to do with interest aggregation, and at times such activity may even undo whatever interest aggregation the party has achieved for election purposes.

Normative linkage has received hardly any attention from the linkage theorists. The political system and within it the various sub-systems such as party organisations presuppose the presence of shared normative perspectives. Normative perspectives, in other words, perform the linkage function within as well as between different systems. The ideals of the common weal are provided by the ruling elite and by the media, as well as by the exponents of the party programmes. These leaders of public opinion evaluate the quality of public life, identify critical issues facing the society as a whole and indicate new directions to take. They also engage in mutual criticism and evaluate competing policy proposals in terms of what would lead to an improved common welfare. This form of linkage activity occurs at a normative level within the community as a whole and the party organisation is but one of many groups involved.

There are occasions in the history of every democratic society when the contribution of the party organisation to normative linkage is minimal. A party organisation can become obsessed with the game of power and the denunciation of adversaries. On such occasions the voter may show more concern for national interest than the party does, and may even endeavour to link himself to the system unaided, if not obstructed, by the party.

A number of cross-national illustrations can be cited in support of this argument. Thinking men and women in the USA, during the summer of 1974, for instance, seemed much more concerned with the quick resolution of the Watergate problem than did the two national political parties, which changed their stance only after the historic decision on the Nixon tapes by the US Supreme Court.

While the political parties were engaged in viewing the Watergate episode from the point of view of its effects on their respective electoral fortunes, concerned citizens were demanding, especially through the media, a cleaner public life, the rule of law and public accountability on the part of the highest office in the country.

In 1971, to cite another illustration, the electorate in India registered its grave national concern over the growing political instability in the country as a result of cynical floor-crossing by elected deputies. It was estimated that between 1967 and 1971 one-third of the total number of elected deputies in the state legislative assemblies and Parliament in India defected from their political parties in return for cash or office. Alarmed by the politics of defection, the electorate in India in the 1971 election returned the ruling Congress Party with a big majority to put an end to the political instability arising out of party desertions. The electoral verdict surprised even the Congress Party. The voters wanted the ruling party to get down to the urgent task of resolving economic problems rather than spending most of its time enticing defectors away from its opponents.

As regards operational linkage,[15] it is necessary to note that in the last analysis what sustains a system of party linkages is the activity of those who direct their energies to the task of building and sustaining a structure of support for their party organisations. While a few among them are drawn to party work as a means to what they think is the public good, the bulk of them undertake such a work for what they can get out of it. These latter seek their reward in the form of power, status or material benefit. Without such a pay-off few would be interested in the linkage work of the parties.

The linkmen involved in operational linkage activity are the office-bearers, the party activists and the 'marginals'. The marginals are the fringe people who periodically get involved in partisan politics. They are not fully assimilated into the party organisations. Nevertheless, the party organisations need their support in order to put across to the widely dispersed electorate, as effectively as possible, the vote-catching items in the party programmes. Apart from a few public-spirited individuals, the marginals make their services available to party organisations in return for potential political advantage to themselves.[16] The greatest single problem for any party organisation is to sustain the interest of its activists and marginals *as* linkmen. Since the party activists and the marginals get involved in extra- and non-party political activity, especially between elections, the consequences of such involvements for party linkages become unpredictable. During the period preceding elections the linkmen build a patchwork of support structure for the party organisation, but between elections they are likely, as we shall see, to join competing support structures which do not necessarily run parallel to the existing party cleavages. The activists and the marginals often cut across such cleavage structures. Neither the activists nor the marginals, with a few exceptions, don the party uniform all the time. Many enter into a dialogue across the party fences as soon as the electoral rhetoric dies down, and erstwhile enemies may form peculiar and sometimes unpredictable political combinations.

Consequently, it is important to examine closely the operational conduct of the activists and the marginals between elections, and more specifically their off-election 'de-membering'. No analysis of linkage activity will be complete unless we also take into account the extra-linkage activity of its linkmen. In many political systems, the activity of linkmen alternates between building up a patchwork of support for electoral strife and then dismantling it for a variety of accommodations at the party and individual levels.

(b)   A model of political party strife-accommodation
In the various writings on party organisation, linkage activity is rarely considered against the background of inter-party behaviour. The activists and the marginals are often considered to be pursuing linkage activity and nothing else. The horsetrading activity between elections, especially across the party fence, is often lost sight of. This is partly due to the fact that party conflict, which figures prominently during electoral contests, is taken far too seriously. Since their mutually exclusive linkages are built out of the gross mass of common potential supporters by stressing points of conflict, the rivalry between the linkmen of contesting political parties is considered to be an ever-present phenomenon. It is therefore not surprising that the phenomenon of inter-party activity has received little or no attention.

Inter-party accommodations: party to party As far as Indian political parties are concerned two scholars have thrown light on some aspects of the phenomenon of accommodation among them. As already noted, they are Myron Weiner and W. H. Morris-Jones. The former underlined the accommodation and close 'fit' between the interests of members and party organisations, whereas the latter spoke of positive communication and interaction between the Congress Party and the other political parties as involved in the process of bargaining and accommodation. This latter approach in fact came fairly close to identifying the endless sequence of political linkages built for electoral strife and inter-party accommodations between elections.

The members of the Congress and the Swatantra Parties at the local level fought their electoral battles with all the wiles, skills and resources at their command. But soon after the elections, the contrived political hostility gave way to an increasing degree of normal sociability and a spirit of give-and-take. Both sides showed extreme unwillingness to pursue a zero-sum-game in which the winners would try and humble the losers in every respect. The political leadership of the Congress as well as the Swatantra Party was drawn from commercial and agriculturist classes where everyone had personally experienced phases of prosperity and lean periods. Consequently, despite continuing bitterness on the part of some of the activists towards their electoral opponents, the bulk of the leaders within both the political parties often explored the areas of party co-operation, particularly in specific fields where a continuing political hostility was considered to be neither a good policy nor helpful to one's image. In the composition of executive committees of various institutions of Anand, for instance, one could often notice a dominant party offering a disproportionate share of seats to its opponents.

Intra-party accommodations: individual to individual The intraparty accommodations at the individual level across the party fence – particularly between individuals of common religious, ethnic, regional or class origins – have received much less attention. No party organisation in a democratic society can impose a formal cast of hostility on the entire range of socio-political relationships which exist between the members of contesting political parties. Despite hostile partisanship, the undercurrent of primary social ties quite often opens up avenues for political accommodations at an individual level. Post-election periods are conducive to the resumption of normal sociability and political accommodation across the party line.

Party cleavages cut across ethnic groups and sometimes the far more cohesive sub-groups within them. Thus, for instance, both the political parties had their leadership drawn from Anand as well as the six *mota gams* of the Patidars. The derision bordering on contempt on the part of the Patidars of the *mota gams* for the Patidars of Anand was well known. This often had a curious effect on the decision-making bodies of the various committees. Whenever elections requiring the mobilisation of party organisations were in the background, the strong Anand sentiment often brought the Patidars across the party divide to take part in the decision-making process together. The same was also true of the Patidars from the *mota gams*.

Extra-party accommodations There are also occasions which give rise to extra-party accommodations. In such situations, political parties are not directly involved in the electoral fray and local party officials may connive at various liaisons and accommodations arranged between supposedly competitive party activists and marginals on the boards of non-partisan institutions.

Both the main political parties allowed a section of their leadership to enter into peculiar deals with each other as long as such commitments did not involve the top party echelons in any politically awkward situations. In various educational, economic and civic bodies of Anand, one could always notice some kind of horsetrading between the two political parties for membership of committees or for specific policies and the extent of their implementation.

Non-party accommodations Finally, there are non-party accommodations. Between elections, several new issues of common concern are likely to develop. Until a partisan approach to such issues crystallises, individuals belonging to different political parties will often enter into situations of mutual accommodation.

The people of Anand had a long tradition of working in various social work organisations. Whenever social workers undertook any specific project, they could always count on active and sometimes joint support from the political leadership of the Congress as well as the Swatantra Parties. The leaders of the two parties often worked together in a spirit of comradeship as long as neither took up a partisan position on any specific issue.

In short, it is important to identify the nature and extent of involvement of party office-bearers, activitists and marginals in situations of inter-party, extra-party and non-party accommodations, together with the significance of such an involvement to the linkage structure itself.

In a sense the politics of accommodation alternates and undercuts the politics of linkage. Since most political parties are essentially electioneering parties, their accent on linkages is revived only during the periods preceding elections. Nevertheless, all accommodations – whether entered into by the parties themselves or by their activists and marginals – merely hasten up the process of dissolution of the patchwork of electoral linkages. At the end of each round of accommodations the parties are often left with their unshaken ideological affiliates and those who habitually refuse to look for political alternatives.

Party-to-party accommodations between the erstwhile competitors are entered into with a veiw either to maximise political advantage or to ensure political survival.[17] The individual-to-individual accommodations and liaisons across the party fence, on the other hand, are brought about with indifference to their long-term effect on the parties' following. Within the support structures themselves the party-to-party accommodations may cause confusion in the minds of people who had swung behind the competitive parties, whereas the get-together at individual level of the former antagonists is often cynically written off as 'politics'.

In democratic political systems which are merely based on *periodic* mandates from the people rather than multifarious accountability, political parties, regardless of their capacity, neither have the incentive nor the urgency – barring a few segments of their traditional support – to guard against the disintegration of their support structures between elections.

During the period between elections, the activists and marginals have time to spare. There is more time and energy for political pursuits in the local unit of a party than is used or demanded by the national body under the party programme. The local unit's unused time, energy and organisational power are available to the people who control, influence or manipulate them. All are used to enter into a variety of political accommodations with uncertain effect on party linkages.

The variety of accommodations discussed here take their own toll of party linkages. Every incidence of accommodation potentially weakens the ties between party personnel, party organisation and party supporters. Party accommodations between elections encourage the movement of some activists and a large number of marginals from one side of the party divide to the other, encourage movement out of party politics altogether, and seriously undermine the linkage structure so laboriously built during the pre-election periods.

II THE ELECTORAL CAMPAIGN

THE INVASION OF THE PRIMARY GROUPS

Earlier we examined in detail the attempts made by party organisations to tap the social cohesion of various castes and their increasing inability to do so. Through the successive elections the parties' instrumental purpose in nominating candidates also changed. With the exception of the Jan Sangh's attempt of appealing to the Patidar voters with the help of a Patidar nominee, the Congress as well as the opposition parties put before the voters candidates who reflected the party's deliberately cultivated image, concerns and programmatic ideas. The parties deeply involved in contest through their nominees were eager to move on to the matters of substance and policy rather than let the nominees work up their own individual and social pulls. In so doing the party organisations put a negative insurance on the social origins of their nominees. The absence of consideration of social origin could harm their electoral prospects if they were not taken care of. The parties, therefore, often sought to neutralise any advantages to each other arising out of a caste of the nominee. For this reason, whenever the need arose, Kshatriyas were pitted against Kshatriyas and Patidars against Patidars. Once that was achieved, the parties quickly moved on to the matters of substance.

Over the years the voters too were sufficiently politically socialised to note that the parties paid attention to the caste of the candidate in so far as it was likely to put them to a great disadvantage *vis-à-vis* their rivals. Thus, whenever the need arose, the factor of the candidate's caste became a vote-catching instrument for a mutually vote-neutralising strategy. Especially during the elections of 1971 and 1972, the contesting sides neutralised each other's suspected advantage among the Kshatriya voters by nominating Kshatriya candidates. Once that was done, the rival parties tried very hard to protect a pro-underdog image and the promise of relief for the poor through their nominees and electoral campaign. These two elections also proved that the more effective the pro-poor image of a party, the greater its electoral returns. The issues which dominated the elections of 1975 and 1977 were cleaner administration and restoration of civil liberties, respectively.

THE INCREASING USE OF THE PAID POLITICAL WORKERS

The growing intensity of electoral contest compelled the party organisations to make provision for the paid political workers who would guard their interests in urban and rural areas of the constituency. The parties needed some insurance against the fickleness of the electoral promises by the voters. Voters who promised their vote to one group of canvassers often changed their minds when the rival group showed up. In order to mend the party fence, prevent electoral drift, fight the temptation of more cash for the 'promise' of votes, and above all to disrupt the meetings of rivals, whenever possible, party organisers employed paid neighbourhood agents. Such agents were the local toughs or activists who were supposed to keep the electoral herd well insulated from the rivals. They were also supposed to resolve doubts in the event of rival penetration.

Such an approach to one's electoral supporters was conceived in the image of one's agricultural crop. The crop that you work for is yours, and needs to be protected more and more when it is ready to be cut. You employ the *rakhas* (hired watchmen) to protect it. The encroachment upon your crop should be defended physically if necessary. In the bitterly contested election of 1971, there were a number of cases of intimidation and violence and, in some cases, loss of life.

THE MOBILISATION OF BUSINESSMEN AND THEIR INFLUENCE

In all the elections great reliance was put by the campaign managers on businessmen. They were approached for funds and assistance in transport and material for propaganda on the one hand, and for their own influence on the business community on the other. In return for their assistance they were promised various kinds of help in administrative matters.

CAMPAIGN SPEECHES BY PROMINENT LEADERS

The campaigns by the candidates, and on their behalf by party stalwarts, were an exercise in periodic political accountability by the sitting member, and an occasion for putting across the relative superiority of the policy proposal of one's party to those proposed by the contestant. Through such an exercise more and more voters were politically socialised and inducted into the electoral process, for it gave them some basic information and the opportunity to make a political choice.

In 1967, the Congress nominee, Narendrasingh Mahida, admitted that the rate of economic development was rather slow but claimed that nevertheless some progress had been made. He put his arguments as follows:

The wars with China and Pakistan, food imports, relief for drought stricken areas had all exhausted whatever little financial surplus there was. Still your [village audience's] present economic condition would compare favourably with what it was fifteen years ago. Then you used to get up early in the morning and walk down to Anand; now you go by bus. Then you could not afford to eat in the town; now you take snacks and tea whenever you are there. Then you could not afford to do any shopping in the town; now you invariably buy a shirt or a pair of sandals or a toy for your child. Then you returned from the town before it got dark; now you invariably see a movie and then return by bus.[18]

Such a comparison had an enormous effect on the audience. The fact that such problems were uppermost in the minds of the voters was borne out by the questions that followed. They all related to the difficulties experienced in obtaining seed, fertiliser, water, loans, and above all the complexities of the laws governing land tenure.

The campaign meeting held by the leader of the Swatantra Party, Bhaikaka, in 1967, attended by prosperous Patidars, also had its own administrative-economic overtones. He came out with a catalogue of economic problems: the foreign debt which India had contracted since independence; stifled activity in agriculture, commerce and industry; unjust land-tenure policy; administrative red-tape and non-decision-making; and how the time was ripe for a change of government. Until the Congress Party was ousted from power, he maintained, those difficulties would continue.[19]

Mrs Gandhi's campaign meeting in 1971 in Anand was attended by nearly 100,000 people, drawn from a radius of forty miles. In her speech she admitted that the main beneficiary of India's economic development since independence was a small segment of the total population. But now new wealth had to be generated, the beneficiary of which would be the average man. The greatest problem facing the country was poverty, she added, and the government under her leadership would devote itself mainly to the task of *garibi hatao* (eradicate poverty).[20]

The elections of 1962 and 1971, to use V.O. Key's expression, were 'critical elections' for the growth of democracy in India. The election of 1962 set into motion and in certain cases crystallised the processes of vote-differentiation among the bulk of the social and religious groups. The election of 1971, on the other hand, brought into the electoral dialogue and opinion formation substantive issues relating to political stability and the economic situation. For a country with as many economic problems as India, the important criterion for judging the performance of the party in power, especially after 1971, was going to be the economic one.

The campaign for the election of 1972 sensitised the electorate to some extent to the need to think in terms of an integrated union-state party government which instead of working at cross-purposes would address itself to the common goals in a concerted fashion.

The campaign for the election of 1975 took place against the background of the Navnirman Movement. The Congress Party accused the opposition of undermining the duly elected legislature, while the Janata openly charged the Congress Party of corruption and failure to hold the price line. Unlike all other previous elections, both sides specifically referred to certain economic measures which they promised to implement if returned to office. Janata also heavily underlined the problem of corruption, the need for severe punishment to all those involved in corrupt practices and the declaration of assets of its members who would be elected to the legislature.

The campaign for the 1977 election was slow to get off the ground. Soon after the announcement of the election the Janata group began to explore the extent of criticism in the electoral campaign that would be permitted by the Congress Party. What electrified the group, and also the electorate, was the publicity given by the newspapers to the increasingly bolder criticism of the Congress administration and repression by the veterans like Morarji Desai, J. P. and Jagjivan Ram. Soon fear of the Congress Party began to melt. The Congress accused the opposition of excesses in agitation and the Janata accused the Congress Party of excesses in its repressive rule in general. While the Congress Party threw into the campaign its enormous resources of men and material and underlined the need for discipline to make India strong, the Janata concentrated on the loss of civil liberties in the Congress *Raj*.

DISTORTIONS, CASH AND RUMOURS

The use of cash to buy votes progressively increased and reached its climax in the election of 1971. That election came at the end of the politics of defection practised on a mass scale. Money was used in order to shrink legislative majorities and form or topple ministries. Financial motives were attributed in public and no one sued anyone for libel. The voter suspected the political worker of having been a mercenary, the political worker suspected the electoral nominee of preparing to sell his vote to the highest bidder inside the legislature, and so forth. Such an atmosphere, in which everybody's motive was suspect, severely restricted the influence of party organisations. Tempted by the cash offered by both sides, harassed into electoral promises, at times by means of ritual oaths, the voter often decided to accept money from whoever was willing to offer it. The acceptance of cash from both sides liberated the voter, as it were, from the obligation to vote for one or the other side because of money. By 1971, the electorate had certainly come of age in the art of using the secret ballot. On the eve of the election of 1971, the Election Commissioner, in a highly publicised statement, gave encouraging assurances on the confidentiality of the vote. Outside the polling booths the political workers often confessed with a sense of frustration their inability to find out where the voter, despite his promises, had actually voted.

Finally, we come to the part played by rumours. There were rumours relating to the defection of the top-level leaders, of various deals that they had entered into across the party line, and above all of the advent of big money from outside to buy votes. In launching rumours of all kinds, the political workers on both sides, during the election of 1971, had played an important part. In a manner of speaking, they used the rumours in order to prepare the voter for a possible defeat of their side. At times the rumours were also used as legitimate weapons in the electoral contest. Despite the fact that the rumours did not always yield the intended results, their first impact on the adversary was quite chilling.

There was also some degree of awareness of the rumours as a

necessary aspect of group behaviour. With great ease the contending groups often described the unwelcome items in the newspapers as *Khoti afva* (rumour).

Like the use of cash, rumours too became neutralised when the contending sides deliberately launched them, leaving the electorate much less influenced than was intended by either side.

HANDBILLS AND NEWSPAPERS

Over the years, a marked difference was noticeable in the content of election handbills and the role of the newspapers. The handbills, apart from their continuing tradition of exposés, addressed themselves more and more to the question of economic policy and administrative performance, and the newspapers took upon themselves the responsibility of furnishing political arguments for the voters sharply divided on party lines. The handbills and the newspapers together reflected the image of a changing electorate who, among other things, had to be approached with the presentation of substantive policy issues in secular, rational terms. The details of those presentations appeared beside various electoral advertisements covering half, and sometimes full pages of the Gujarati newspapers. At times electoral advertisements also appeared in the newspapers which subscribed to the views of the rival party. Such advertisements furnished an insight into a party organisation's view that they were approaching a clientèle which was rapidly growing in political sophistication.

The campaign literature which appeared on behalf of the Congress Party during the election of 1967 spoke of the achievements of the party during the past two decades in the field of irrigation, electricity, public works, education, agricultural production, price control, defence, etc. Despite heavy odds, it claimed, the country had made a good beginning in those areas. The Swatantra Party literature, on the other hand, was critical of excessive policy restrictions slowing down the pace of economic activity, the vast increase in administrative expenses, the enormous public debt, and spoke of the need to change government in the interests of democracy.

In the following election, coming in the wake of a bitter split in the Congress Party, a touch of acrimony crept into the handbills as well as the Party write-ups, along with the economic arguments. A considerable portion of election material was devoted to reviling the other side. The Organisation Congress in Gujarat, during the election of 1971, led the offensive. It came out with campaign literature which was nearly ten times the volume of that of the Ruling Congress. The literature was largely devoted to accusing Mrs Gandhi of having disrupted the unity of the Congress Party. Morarji Desai, who was deeply involved in a bitter struggle for power, specially prepared a pamphlet in English under the title *Facts You Must Know*. It concluded on the following note:

> The ruling party has embarked on a path of indiscipline, patronage, nepotism and corruption which led to dictatorship of one kind or another. It is the duty of the Congress [Organisation Congress] and of all democratic parties to fight these growing forces of disruption and dictatorship.[21]

The handbills defending the Ruling Congress accused the other side of encouraging a party like the Jan Sangh, some of whose organisers had been involved in the assassination of Gandhi. They claimed that the Jan Sangh had instigated some of the communal riots in Gujarat, probably the worst since independence, and that in the final analysis it was a fascist party.

On the more positive side the Ruling Congress asked the voter to give his mandate so that it would boldly implement its programme of basic social change. The write-ups on behalf of the Ruling Congress devoted much less space to party polemics and much more to substantive issues. Judging from the election results, the party's positive approach to problems seemed to be well received by the voters.

The qualitative change in the election literature of 1971 reflected the great strides made by the electorate in the perception of issues. Since everywhere there were discussions and arguments preceding the elections, the contesting parties were induced to bring out arguments which were easily digestible and which could be repeated by their supporters. Since both sides had come armed with such material, it indicated a shift in the parties' strategy towards the changing electorate. The party organisers could no longer merely depend on the leaders of the primary groups: those of neighbourhood, kin group, and caste. The Indian electorate, over the years, had become relatively more demanding. It now wanted the presentation of party programmes and arguments in support of them. Such a presentation had now become more than a mere election ritual. In addition, the electorate often sought replies to its queries and clarification of its doubts. In terms of an emerging political culture the bulk of the electorate was in a position to *talk* on political problems without seeming to become discourteous or fearing the consequent social ostracism.

The discriminating capacity of the electorate continued to grow. In deference to that, the Janata group brought out, in 1975, a short flyer, over and above its ponderous manifesto, pointing out at a glance what it was pledging to do. Most of the points mentioned in it had already become part of the electoral dialogue. The Janata thus offered itself to be judged by the electorate on highly specific issues.

Like the campaign literature, the newspapers also reflected the qualitative change that had occurred in the electorate. In certain cases the correlation between the newspapers and vote-intention was also observable. Day after day the newspapers went on feeding a maturing electorate with specific arguments, perspectives and a rationale for its proposed political choice.

III VOTER CONTACT

One of the most intractable problems of Indian electoral politics is the way in which the party organisations contact voters. Their contact often involves, among other things, the use of a complex network of inter-personal relationships which surround the voter. Party organisations explore the possibility of converting the influence structure implicit in any form of relationship in to an electoral influence. Consequently, any research in this area has to depend on our educated guesses and hunches as to the type of intermediaries used by party organisations to obtain the desired influence.

Apart from getting election literature to the voter, party agents in Anand often tried to interest him in listening to campaign speeches given by their effective speakers. Then, individually, they contacted the voter by means of effective intermediaries.

As far as the individual voter was concerned, he could be reached by means of one or more of the following intermediaries (see Table 5.1):

TABLE 5.1.   1967 General Election: party intermediaries employed to bring in the vote

Caste/ religion	Party worker	Employer	Caste/ religious leader	Neighbour- hood leader	Co-worker	No one
Brahmins	8	–	3	–		23
Banias	7	–	–	2		16
Patidars	13	–	4	6		78
Kshatriyas	14	–	9	5		89
Christians	2	–	–	1		28
Muslims	1	–	–	–		20

the party worker;
his employer;
his caste leader;
his neighbourhood leader;
his co-worker.

Viewed from the point of view of the growing maturity in voting the choice of intermediary reflected the following electoral character:

party worker: represents specific political purpose;
co-worker: reflects diversity of social background of co-workers; political discussion and persuasion;
neighbourhood leader: represents the extension of primary group influence on electoral choice;
employer: represents an element of constraint;
caste or religious leader: indicates an appeal to social solidarity.[22]

TABLE 5.2.   1971 General Election: party intermediaries employed to bring in the vote

Caste/ religion	Party worker	Employer	Caste/ religious leader	Neighbour- hood leader	Co-worker	No one
Brahmins	1					31
Banias	3					23
Patidars	3					100
Kshatriyas	34			18	1	68
Christians	4				1	22
Muslims	2					19

Between the two elections of 1967 and 1971 there was a remarkable drop in the use of caste and religious leaders as intermediaries by the party organisations. During the election of 1971, particularly, the party organisers realised for the first time the futility of influencing voters through the old and venerated caste and religious leaders (see Table 5.2). Other leaders who acted as intermediaries made their contact with the voters, by and large, in a political capacity for a specific political purpose.

Fewer party workers cared to contact the voters of the upper castes such as the Brahmins, Banias and Patidars. But when it came to the Kshatriyas, they were individually canvassed in a big way. From the point of view of the party workers, the voters in the upper castes had been already inducted into the political process, leaving little or no scope for persuasion by the party intermediaries. Finally, only the Kshatriyas indicated the use of neighbourhood leaders to canvass them. In the party organisations' assessment of the influence structure operating among the Kshatriyas, therefore, the neighbourhood leaders seemed to play a relatively more important role.

A great change was noticeable in the canvassing techniques of party organisations after the election of 1971. All the parties extensively contacted voters by means of party workers. Between 1971 and 1972 the number of voters canvassed by means of party workers rose considerably. On the eve of the 1972 election a substantial number of voters claimed that their vote was canvassed, individually or in groups, by the party workers. There was thus an obvious decline in reliance on influential people within the groups by party organisations when it came to their own political survival. Correspondingly, the shift in the party organisations' approach to the voter also reflected their growing respect for the political understanding and discriminating choice of the electorate.

On the eve of the election of 1975, the reliance of the party organisations on party workers, as opposed to the neighbourhood or ethnic intermediaries, continued in a big way (see Table 5.3). Among those who cast their votes, only 4 per cent were canvassed by means of such intermediaries. Among such voters, the Congress Party had concentrated on the Christians and the Muslims, the Janata had concentrated on the Brahmins and the Patidars, and the KMLP on the Banias, Patidars and Christians.

The proportion of voters canvassed by party workers in 1975 more than doubled. Among other things this indicated an

TABLE 5.3.   1975 General Election: party intermediaries employed to bring in
the vote

Caste/ religion	Party worker	Employer	Caste/ religious leader	Neighbour- hood leader	Co-worker	No one
Brahmins	15			1	–	21
Banias	12	1	2		–	12
Patidars	31		9		–	67
Kshatriyas	51		9	3	–	71
Christians	12	2	3		–	12
Muslims	12		5		–	24

increasingly keener contest for votes among the political parties.
The party workers were forced to rely less and less on means other
than their own contact with the voters.

6 An Emerging Political Society

Democratic institutions are easy to establish but difficult to sustain. They can be formally set up by means of constitutional provisions and their implementations. But to sustain them, and the democratic process in general, what is required is a political society which shares their underlying values and constantly manifests commitment to them in its own political activity. Only such a political society, as de Tocqueville pointed out in *Democracy in America*, can ensure the operation of the democratic process and the survival of its institutions.

Historically speaking, the growth of political societies in the Western countries, which have been able to ensure the survival of their democratic institutions, has taken two to three centuries to evolve. Such political societies emerged as a result of innumerable changes in their economy and social organisation and the consequent demand within them for the reorganisation of legal and political institutions.

Such a sequence and time-span, so far as the developing countries are concerned, has been reversed. In these countries several attempts have been made to establish democratic institutions first, often by triumphant nationalist leaders in the euphoric moment of national independence, and they hope, rather than actively strive, for the quickest possible growth of commensurate political societies. In the majority of such countries civilian or military dictatorships have superseded the democratic political institutions.

Among the developing countries, despite her manifold problems, India has been one of the very few to evolve the kind of political society needed to protect her democratic institutions. In a sense the evolution of her political society, which was destined to play a part in sustaining her democratic institutions, begun long before she attained her independence. Her prolonged freedom struggle, the calibre of her nationalist leaders and their commitment to democratic values, and above all the assimilation of such values by the growing educated middle class, gave a head start to the development of such a political society. Nevertheless, the crucial aspects developed after her independence and more particularly during the critical periods of doubt, ineffectiveness and deliberate inroads into its liberal structure by Indira Gandhi. In the emerging political society of India certain aspects have crystallised sufficiently to give direction to her democratic process. Whereas others, still in the process of overcoming their internal contradictions, often tend to pull in different directions, giving an overall impression of political instability or even what John Kenneth Galbraith called 'organised anarchy'. Such destabilising aspects have not succeeded in placing India's democratic process off course. In this chapter we shall examine their operative significance to India's emerging political society, discussing in turn the concept of a political society, secular orientations, her political mobilisation and its far-reaching consequences and specific political attitudes, and ending with a profile of the political society that is emerging there.

I POLITICAL SOCIETY

In the 1960s, two of the most powerful concepts in political development to gain currency were 'civic culture' and 'political culture'. Almond and Verba in *The Civic Culture: Political Attitudes in Democracy in Five Nations* (1963)[1] used the concept of 'civic culture' to analyse the political orientations of the relatively more stable political societies. And Pye, Verba *et al*, in *Political Culture and Political Development* (1965)[2] used the concept 'political culture' to examine the peculiarities of the political orientations of a number of developing countries which, due to their culture and tradition, had manifested political traits which had set them apart from the political systems of the Western world. Both these terms, in a manner of speaking, had been used in order to refer to political orientations of different societies as *settled*. The word 'culture', which is common to both of them, implies a settled behavioural pattern with its own implicit or explicit system of values.[3] In his paper 'India: Two Political Cultures', Myron Weiner suggested that both the mass political culture and the elite political culture had different proportions of the traditional and the modern components in them.[4] Apart from the insoluble mix of the new and the old in the two political cultures, what was indeed difficult to accept in such a characterisation was the *settled* traits of Indian political culture, one or more than one. What is in evidence, on the other hand, are a few emerging peculiarities of the Indian democratic process, in the field of her political society, where the individuals, tied to the network of primary groups to which they were born, are forced to make choices on secular matters by identifying themselves with personalities, issues, party organisations or interest groups. Such peculiarities have not yet acquired, in my view, the settled character of a 'political culture'. Nor are the seemingly irreconcilable contradictions, simultaneously affirming and rejecting certain political positions, ironed out. Nevertheless, together such peculiarities and contradictions do constitute a matrix within which India's political society is likely to evolve.

No political society can be lastingly built on the settled political traits of a people, simply because no people in history have ever possessed finally and fully settled political traits. Certain political traits which helped them to sustain a set of political practices today may become inadequate tomorrow, thus forcing them either to adapt to the change or explore new ways of regaining their political adequacy. Thus, for instance, the civic virtues based on certain political traits, developed in the West in the pre-electronic age, have had difficulty in keeping the essentials of democratic process intact in an age which makes limitless use of sophisticated media. Then there is the growing menace of the inordinate influence exerted by corporate power – big unions, big governments, etc. – which makes political practices based on old-fashioned civic virtues appear inadequate. Finally, there are the inroads made by leisure and the leisure industry into a citizen's free time, which prevent or compete with his possible involvement in the democratic process. Only in a relative sense, therefore, can one talk about some political traits as more developed than others, and they must continually face the test of their own adequacy in any political society.

TABLE 6.1. Political society

Social organisation and economic structure into which individuals are born	Political society: The arena where politically mobilised individuals join secular collectivities of party organisations, unions or interest groups to pursue their political goals.	Legal and political institutions

A political society occupies a position between social organisation and economic structure on the one hand, and legal and political institutions on the other (see Table 6.1). It is an arena where people born to certain ethnic, religious and class groupings make efforts to build or join secular collectivities of political parties, unions and interest groups, with a cross-section of people to influence and control public instituions. It is the product of a continuing interaction between social and cultural conditions, goal directions, mobilisation processes and participatory involvements, and above all a constantly emerging pattern of political behaviour which influences and conditions a part of the subsequent political activity. People who play a part in political society develop a capacity for working with those who do not share their ethnicity, religion or class, or even ideology. Together they address themselves either to specific issues which agitate their minds or affect their interests, or forge new political bonds within party organisations and interest groups in order to build enduring bases of political support for their continuing political objectives.

A political society also shares an implicit-explicit set of values which encourage and deter certain kinds of political action. At critical moments of invoking public involvement or of warning it against a possible breach of the democratic process, such values become articulated and the conduct of public men and the performance of public institutions come under increasing scrutiny. Such values require the individual in the political society to make a decision, after careful scrutiny, as to whether to give or to renew his mandate to govern to competing candidates during periodic elections. Finally, such values also put limitations on his political activity, indicating how and by what means a mandate to govern can be given, a new political authority can be constituted, and the rights of those in and out of public office can be exercised.

Such a normative structure of a political society, which sustains its democratic process, nevertheless does not always remain inviolate. Emotional issues, intensity of political conflicts, excesses of authority and opposition, and above all continued inability to secure response to legitimate demands often lead to a breach of the democratic process. But what makes democratic systems stable is not the total absence of a breach of the democratic process itself but an unfailing resurgence from such a breach and the reaffirmation of its basic values. In other words, whenever its fragile protective armour gives in, its recuperative energy, with its source in the deep commitment to democratic values within a political society, helps it to revive the democratic process. That was what was noticeable in the anti-Vietnam agitations and Watergate in the USA and the political agitations of 1968 in France. There were breaches of the democratic process and resurgence of it in both those countries.

So far India has withstood severer tests of a breach of her democratic process in recent years than the relatively more stable democracies of the West. Nor can there be any doubt that, given the immensity of her problems, further infractions of her democratic process will be attempted. The basic question, then, is whether certain fundamental aspects in her political society have firmed up enough to ensure a revival, in case of future onslaughts, of her democratic process. To that we now turn.

II SECULAR ORIENTATIONS

The elite, party organisations, unions, interest groups and social work agencies in India seek to mobilise people in support of their standpoint within her political society. For specific purposes, each of the mobilised individuals is, so to speak, drawn *out* of the ethnic group to which he was born and the productive relationships within which he made his living. The individuals and organisations who mobilise them, in order to gather support for their demands, seek to build cross-ethnic, cross-occupational, secular groups within the political society. For their primary social concerns and their means of livelihood, however, the mobilised individuals continue to be members of their ethnic and occupational groups. While such groups remain cohesive, passive and undemanding in their primary social and occupational concerns, those individuals within them, when mobilised into the political society, are persuaded to act within the framework of cleavage, demand and political pressure. What the mobilisers within the political society aim at is to persuade such individuals to play a political role by virtue of their contact with political organisations or interest groups or unions, without ceasing to be members of their primary social and occupational groups.

An uninhibited operation of the democratic process presupposes the possibility of secular mobilisation of individuals, regardless of the tightly knit cohesive social groups to which they belong. In a span of about a quarter of a century, through successive General Elections, as we have seen in Chapter 2, India was able to build a secular political society which was able to make the operation of the democratic process within it possible. As the socially cohesive citizens of India went through her democratic mill, they also learned to make a distinction between the realm of primary social concern and that of secular democratic politics. For a traditional and slow-moving society this was indeed a great step forward.

Relatively speaking, India has had less success in building secular collectivities in the form of economic interest groups. As we have seen in Chapter 3, in certain cases the social priorities of the poor preceded their economic priorities. In that connection, we examined the sequentiality of social humiliation and poverty. The poor in India also became obsessed with the social considerations of their humiliating position in the social hierarchy and, therefore, paid more attention to its removal with the help of their ethnic groups rather than by joining secular collectivities within the political society and generating much more effective political pressure towards their economic demands. It still remains for the ethnic class or the occupational class of their birth to be replaced by a secular class which could be the basis of a union or interest group and a much-needed political militancy.

The three electoral generations that we examined in Chapter 4 presented much less difficulty of secular orientation within Indian political society. This was because, while generational perspectives and evaluations differed, the formation of secular collectivities consisting of a cross-section of them within party organisations stimulated dialogue and the exploration of alternatives. It also combined the experience and commitment of the old with the idealism and energy of the young. In a sense the Navnirman protest movement in Gujarat and the tremendous electoral campaign waged by the Janata movement in 1977 were the products of such generational combinations.

Different factors within ethnicity, class and generation, however, create conditions which inhibit or facilitate the individual's participation in secular society. Across these three, the individuals who belonged to ethnic groups which were not obsessed with either the problem of higher social recognition or the retention of their religious identity, who had moved away from the occupations of their birth to more lucrative occupations which their business acumen or acquired skills had made possible, and who were exposed to a widespread emphasis on political participation, constituted a group that was potentially the most likely to become involved in the democratic process within the political society. At the other extreme was the group which depended on ethnic cohesion for its cultural identity and higher social recognition, which more or less pursued the occupations of its birth without joining secular interest groups to improve its economic conditions, and which, in terms of its generational perceptions, was far removed from the mainstream of the political life of its times.

Between these two extremes, however, there were a variety of combinations where different backgrounds of ethnicity, class and generation made all the difference to one's involvement in the political society.

Within the ethnic groups of Brahmins, Banias and Patidars, which already had a higher social recognition within the traditional hierarchy, those who had been pursuing their traditional occupations had much less interest in the democratic process than those among them who had registered some degree of occupational mobility. There again, the segment within those who pursued traditional occupations which was able to appreciate the significance of the democratic process to its own economic interests was likely to be more active within the political society. Of these two active groups, the one with traditional occupational pursuits often depended on old stalwarts for leadership. Such stalwarts also had connections with men of influence and power in the party organisations. The group with occupational mobility, on the other hand, depended more on the leadership given by their interest groups.

Even within the religious groups, occupational mobility made a great deal of difference to one's forging of bonds with a cross-section of people and to joining secular collectivities to protect one's economic interests, and through them, to participating in the democratic process in general. Earlier in this connection we had examined the case of the Vohras, among the Muslims, who as grain merchants had been active in their interest associations and to some extent in the political society itself.

Within the ethnic group of the Kshatriyas, where the search for a higher social recognition had not been fully relegated into the background, political leadership and emphasis on involvement in the democratic process came from those who had registered occupational mobility. The bulk of its leaders had been businessmen, schoolteachers or civil servants. Within the ethnic group itself such leaders were relative newcomers. Its earlier leadership had consisted of the feudal elements which had, by and large, insulated it from the political society. With the shift in its leadership, its internal divisiveness and involvement in the political process also increased. After the change in its leadership, even the differentiated generational perspectives within the group began to acquire political significance.

Ethnicity, class and generation, in other words, acquired their own significance with reference to the individual's role in political society. The social status of his ethnic group, his occupational mobility within or across class, and his perspectives on the democratic process itself, made all the difference to his participation in the political society.

III POLITICAL MOBILISATION AND ITS FAR-REACHING CONSEQUENCES

In a sense India is one of the most politically mobilised societies in the world. This was partly due to her prolonged nationalist movement and the deliberate involvement of her masses in it under the leadership of Mahatma Gandhi at the end of the First World War. Since then, more and more people have been involved in the political process. After independence, for electoral campaigns or the organising of public support for new programmes or for denouncing government policies and performance, political mobilisation was considered by her elite as well as the masses as necessary and legitimate. Only for a short period, preceding the state of emergency declared in 1976, was the legitimacy of the agitational political mobilisation questioned by the then rulers.

In *No Easy Choice: Political Participation in Developing Countries*, Huntington and Nelson argued that mobilised political participation may not always suit the interests of the entrenched elite and it may even regard the involvement of people in the political process as an anti-goal.[5] In India since her independence, however, such an eventuality has not arisen. The Indian political elite regarded political mobilisation of men, and through them of resources, as a good thing. Until adverse results started pouring in, even Indira Gandhi, who called the fateful election of 1977, looked upon it in this way, as a means of legitimising and institutionalising her manifold inroads into the Indian democratic structure.

Political mobilisation, and in particular electoral mobilisation, can be seen as the continuation of the various processes set in motion by the Indian national movement and the prolonged demand, made by subject India on the British *Raj*, to let her constitute an unrestricted political authority based on universal adult suffrage. Political mobilisation and participation by means of elections has since remained an article of faith with Indians. It, in fact, embodies the quintessence of their demand for self-government.

The founding fathers of the Indian republic, in particular Jawaharlal Nehru, and after him Jayaprakash Narayan and Balwantrai Mehta, who formulated the concept of democratisation of rural India, placed an enormous faith in the democratic process itself. By means of democratic institutions at various levels in rural India they had hoped to evoke enough popular interest to cause ferment in a society which was so slow to change, and thereby bring about the possibility of an ever-increasing degree of participation in the task of nation-building.

Several electoral campaigns and the ritual of promises at the time of elections, party literature and personal attempts to put across why a certain policy was or was not implemented, and above all the questioning and heckling of politicians, helped more and more people to discover the significance of elections to their *own* interests and welfare. Their mobilisation, in other words, set in motion certain processes whereby elections could no longer be treated as instruments of marshalling support for the purposes of the electioneering candidates only. The people who were mobilised also began to treat elections as occasions for seeking explanation and solutions of specific problems of their region, and above all giving notice that their continued support could not be taken for granted.

Political mobilisation has thus become an increasingly two-way process. On the one hand, it has mobilised people from their primary social groups into a secular political society where the choice of deputies and policies, affecting everybody's interest and welfare, regardless of primary group origin, has to be made within the framework of party cleavage. On the other hand, each successive election has made the electorate more and more discriminating and demanding and thus turned the individual from a mere voter, whose support could be bought for a little cash and vague promises, into an electoral participant. The emergence of the latter reflected the growing consciousness of the very instrumentality of elections. Elections had ceased to be mere charades in which voters were periodically lined up in support of one's entry into Assembly or Parliament and had increasingly become critical occasions in the electorate's continuing attempt to make their voice heard and the conduct of the elected deputy accountable to them. Over the years the Indian electorate had thus grown in political understanding and capacity.

The central issue for any political society aiming at sustaining its democratic political institutions, is how to enable citizens to exercise control and influence on their elected representatives and thus secure their responsiveness. While those who are elected often wish to dodge such a responsibility, the political activists among the citizens try to secure their accountability at least on the broad issue of policy and its implementation. Since no form of government can become totally responsive to its citizens, says Robert Dahl, the term 'democracy' should be treated only as an ideal type. What we actually have in most of the liberal societies of the West, then, is a different degree of accountability on the part of those who are elected. Dahl, therefore, coined the term 'polyarchy' or 'near democracy'[6] in order to refer to the phenomenon of less than full political accountability.

The responsiveness of the elected to the electorate in India was, for a long time, non-existent. Increased political competitiveness gradually compelled the country's elected representatives to recognise such a responsibility. There again, powerful vested interests and the rich agriculturists were the first to receive a response. So far as the average citizen was concerned, he had to resort either to mass protest movements or to the threat of them to be able to make a political impression on his elected deputy.

The mobilised political society of India has so far gone through its first political crisis, that of accountability. The events preceding the declaration of the state of emergency, its rationalisation and the subsequent reaffirmation of political rights by those who challenged it constituted the first political crisis. The election of 1977 and the grounds for dismantling the institutionalised provisions of the emergency have together theoretically affirmed and factually demonstrated that the citizen of India has the legitimate right to scrutinise the performance of his elected deputies, put pressure on them to explain their public conduct, compel them to heed citizens' demands, and when all that fails, turn them out of office. While the right to a political alternative was all along recognised and even conceded so far as state elections were concerned, for the first time, in 1977, a party such as the Congress, an entrenched successor to the British *Raj*, was thrown out of office against the background of a massive debate on performance in office, repressive measures and the persistent refusal to be adequately accountable.

The continuing mobilisation within the political society, it is logical to assume, will give rise to yet another crisis, that of distribution. Ever since the inception of the Indian republic the principal beneficiaries of her democratic process have been those who were already better off, and, therefore, in a position to get more out of it. The process of political emulation, the overwhelming advantage of numbers and above all the extension of the instrumental use of the democratic process for a wider purpose, will inevitably lead to further political mobilisation for securing a fair share of economic opportunity for the poor. Such a process would have been accelerated had there been a corresponding mobilisation towards the unionisation of the rural poor. The bulk of these are still locked in the occupational class of their birth and, therefore, are unable to form secular collectivities that can generate adequate political pressure. A part of what they have missed for want of unionisation they may yet secure through the implementation of public policy. Most of the political parties in India are at least theoretically committed to socialism and to the eradication of poverty. As the elected deputies did not easily give in to the demand for accountability, they and their party organisations will not easily be compelled to live up to their own professions of socialism. No party organisation will thoughtlessly risk incurring the displeasure of rural and urban vested interests by actually implementing what it has professed in the name of socialism, unless an effective mobilisation forces it to realise what indeed are the chances of its own political survival election after election. For the electorate the distribution crisis may prove to be tougher and more prolonged than the accountability crisis that preceded it.[7]

IV SOME SPECIFIC POLITICAL ATTITUDES

Within the broad framework of the emerging political society of India, certain specific attitudes have begun to crystallise. They refer to an appreciation of the significance of democracy on the part of a society which was plagued by problems of hierarchy, poverty, divisiveness and fear of government. They also refer to a growing emphasis on strong government *within* a democratic framework.

SHOULD *LOKSHAHI* BE ABOLISHED?

The question of the validity of the democratic system in India was raised following the crop of short-lived coalitions which caused so much chaos in various states of India after 1967. The slow rate of economic development and the mounting hardships as a result of the inability of the political system to function adequately, added fuel to the controversy, and finally, the question was being raised against the background of the tragedy of Bangladesh, where the spurning of the demand for basic human rights had resulted in a rebellion and armed conflict.

Lokshahi (democracy) in India had been the basic condition of an overall unity and political stability for a quarter of a century. It progressively inducted into the system the relatively underprivileged actions of society, brought the regional differences and diversity of demand for economic inputs within the framework of give-and-take, gave birth to a social conscience for formulating policies to help the poorer sections and compelled the governmental authority to accept its obligation to implement such policies; it also avoided a head-on collision with religious and social groups while creating conditions whereby they would matter less and less outside the areas of their traditional concern.

The voter response, in 1972, to the question of whether or not *lokshahi* should be abolished was as set out in Table 6.2.

TABLE 6.2. The abolition of *Lokshahi*: percentage voter response, 1972

Should lokshahi be abolished?	No	Yes	Be made to produce results	Do not know
	87	0·58	5	7

It was indeed remarkable to find out that less than 1 per cent of the voters subscribed to the view that *lokshahi* sould be abolished. It was equally interesting to note that only 5 per cent of voters expressed their dissatisfaction at the slowness with which it produced results. There were, in fact, three freak answers, two from the Patidars and one from the Kshatriyas which called for an end to *lokshahi*.

Within the overall acceptance of *lokshahi*, the ground for voting for a particular party alternated between the 'one that will provide good administration' and the 'one that will help the poor'. The two relatively prosperous groups, Banias and Patidars, overwhelmingly indicated that good administration was possible even in a *lokshahi* provided one voted for the right party. The relatively prosperous Brahmins joined the Kshatriyas, Christians and Muslims in asserting that within *lokshahi* the right kind of political party could also help the poor. Thus, *lokshahi* was favoured both by the economically independent and the economically dependent. Most of the controversies on both sides were about policies and the people who implemented them and not about the form of government.

Such an explicit response also indicated that *lokshahi* was no longer an *imposed* political system or a system which merely rested on the historic moral choice of an elite which came into prominence in the course of the struggle for independence, sat on the Constituent Assembly of free India, but did not live to see some of the severest tests through which it passed. On the other hand, *lokshahi* introduced a process which periodically involved the people in elections, and, despite limited political accountability, forced political parties to seek a fresh mandate. It carried into the political system the vivid picture of the condition and dissatisfaction of the masses. It also forced ministers and political workers to go to the people and explain why they could not keep their promises. Above all, *lokshahi* with each new election regenerated the hope and confidence of the people as regards better performance of the system. For the bulk of the voters, therefore, the alternative to *lokshahi* became less and less conceivable.

In a sense the Navnirman Movement was an attempt to put pressure on *lokshahi* to produce results rather than abolish it. Similarly, the rejection of the Congress Party in the election of 1977 was a clear indication of the voter's preference for *lokshahi* regardless of its administrative or economic performance. In the early 1970s, if not before, as our data suggest, the commitment of the average Indian voter to *lokshahi* was beyond dispute. It was such a commitment which revived it despite Mrs Gandhi's deep onslaught on its liberal structure during the period of the state of emergency.

IS STRONG GOVERNMENT NEEDED? WHO CAN GIVE IT?

The question of legitimacy of the democratic political system directly led to the question of the adequacy of its performance. The respondents were asked if the effectiveness of the democratic system would increase if it firmly implemented its own policies. If so, then which particular party was most likely to do so?

The question was posed in 1971, when Mrs Gandhi's emergence as a powerful leader was a remote possibility, and in various states the coalition governments were the very pictures of compromise, softness and administrative corruption. The voter response to the twin-question is shown in Table 6.3.

TABLE 6.3.   The question of strong governments: voter response, 1971

	Yes	*No*
Is strong government needed?	82%	18%
Which party can give it?	%	
The Ruling Congress	48	
The Organisation Congress	42	
The Jan Sangh	7	
No one	3	

On this particular question the two Congress parties became indistinguishable in the voter's mind. The Ruling as well as the Organisation Congress had leaders with a great deal of potential for firmness: Mrs Gandhi and Morarji Desai. In their choice of a party which could be firm, however, the six major social and religious groups displayed a class bias. The firmness expected of the Ruling Congress was different from that of the Organisation Congress. The former was expected to come out with state-interventionist-type firmness which suited the economically less prosperous groups such as the Kshatriyas, Christians and Muslims. The bulk of the relatively well-off Brahmins, Banias and Patidars on the other hand, indicated their preference for the firm implementation of policy proposals which would leave a great scope for their entrepreneurial activity.

The preference for firmness of government on the part of 82 per cent of the electorate was quite significant. Underlying this, there was an assumption that the effectiveness of democratic institutions would be seriously jeopardised if they did not learn to be firm.

V PROFILE OF AN EMERGING POLITICAL SOCIETY

The political society of India has now evolved certain aspects which are capable of giving directions to many areas of her future political growth. At the same time, however, there are other aspects which remain unclear, reflect uncertainty, and may even be considered to be self-contradictory. In the following pages we shall have a closer look at them.

The operation of the democratic process, over the last three decades, has now established a fundamental principle relating to India's political authority. That is, that there is no other way to constitute political authority except by means of *elections*, and that political power in India flows through the ballot box. That principle has been tested both by its persistence and by its resurgence after a potential breach. Ever since the establishment of the Indian republic, political parties of all shades of ideological persuasion have taken for granted that the only legitimate means for their men to enter public institutions and wield political power is through the ballot box. The only time, since Indian independence, when a breach of such a principle was likely to be committed was during the Emergency when Indira Gandhi took upon herself the right to decide whether or not there should be another election. Her official reasons were that elections might merely distract the people from their task of solving India's basic problems. During the initial period of emergency rule she did not bother about the question of legitimacy of her policies as long as she was not in violation of the awesome emergency provisions of the constitution. Whatever was not thus available to her she obtained by means of extraordinary rulings and support for them by her political party in Parliament. In certain cases she did not even hesitate to compel the judiciary to toe her line. But the want of legitimacy made her feel uneasy, given the strong attachment of Indians to the concept of democracy and the social climate it had created in India since the early days of the national movement. Consequently, even she felt the need to legitimise her actions by means of an election. To achieve her goal Indira Gandhi hoped to run a convenient election by partially but not totally relaxing the Emergency and thereby reminding the people of the possible reprisals if support for her was not forthcoming. She thus hoped to make use of the traditional Indian *fear of government*. But she had miscalculated the degree of anger which her policies had caused and the growth of Indian political capacity to make judicious use of the ballot box. By calling an election, regardless of her motives, even Indira Gandhi ended up by strengthening the fundamental political belief in India that the only legitimate way of constituting political authority was by means of an electoral mandate.

The democratic process in India had established yet another basic principle, namely that of an orderly change of government. For one generation of Indians in the 1970s, such an occurrence had taken place for the second time. First, when the British *Raj* had ended in an orderly fashion as a result of the mounting political pressure from inside as well as outside. And, second, when the deeply entrenched Congress *Raj*, the heir to the British, also ended equally peacefully. The fears of a disorderly change were present on both these occasions. In 1947, on the eve of the departure of the British troops from India, a lot of Indians had wildly speculated that they would return through the back door. Similarly, it was also feared, although much less so, that Indira Gandhi might not consider the results of the 1977 election as binding.

The peaceful change of government, brought about by means of a massive political mobilisation in 1977, demonstrated to the people how a government could be changed. So far a change of government in the centre, and especially one like Indira Gandhi's, which towards the end had stifled more civil liberties and expressions of criticism than occurred under the British *Raj*, was only a remote theoretical possibility. The doubts about its actual displacement had led to a lot of political frustration and to protests that verged on violence.

The possibility of bringing about a peaceful change of government, with the help of an adequate political mobilisation, opened up an era of political self-help for the Indians. After 1977, they did not have to explore other forms of government which might be more suitable. What they needed instead was the political will to build up effective pressure, by means of political mobilisation, so as to secure an adequate response from their rulers. They now realised that the men in office had no inherent right to be there; that such men were given the mandate to govern only because of their policy commitments and promises at the time of elections. It was, therefore, quite legitimate to remind them of those commitments and of the possible non-renewal of such a mandate next time around.

With the departure of Indira Gandhi from office, and her defeat in her own constituency, the era of towering individuals in Indian politics also came to an end. In a sense, the introduction of the democratic process in independent India was a continuation of the Indian national movement. To people like Nehru, the winning of independence, the launching of the democratic process, and, above all, the undertaking of the task of the social and economic reconstruction of India, could all be brought about only by building massive *movements*. And by implication such massive movements also needed towering individuals like Mahatma Gandhi, Jawaharlal Nehru, Sardar Patel, Lal Bahadur Shastri, and Indira Gandhi. That concept began to lose its appeal during Indira Gandhi's years in office. The first split in the Congress Party, engineered by Mrs Gandhi in 1969, made her appear as a shrewd political manipulator, who would like to hang on to power rather than being a leader of her people like some of her great predecessors in the Congress Party. Added to that there was her attempt to favour and protect her own son, Sanjay, a failing which even the most politically illinformed could not forgive. Long before her defeat, therefore, in the eyes of the average Indian Indira Gandhi had ceased to be a towering leader.

Right from Raja Rammohan Roy down to Lal Bahadur Shastri, generations of Indians had become used to their leaders being individuals of great stature who were ready to make personal sacrifices in order to play their part in public life. Such a phenomenon had raised the expectations of the Indians inordinately high. Indira Gandhi, and several other politicians who deserted their political parties for political or financial considerations, convinced the Indians that their expectations of the conduct of men in politics was a little too idealistic; that very few in public life would shun personal or family gain; that what was needed was not only righteous anger and condemnation, but also vigilance, scrutiny, exposure, legal action and the constant threat of political alternatives.

The Emergency and its aftermath was a tremendous lesson in democratic political education, both for those in power and for those in opposition. Before the Emergency, the opposition had entertained the hope of being able to dislodge a duly constituted government from power by means of massive protest movements. And during the Emergency the party in power had hopes of putting to permanent disadvantage all political opposition. Both sides had clearly realised that they had overstepped the limits of political action and the exercise of political authority which make the democratic process possible; that unless such limitations to political action were duly acknowledged by both sides, the democratic process itself will be in serious jeopardy.

Both the Congress and the Janata Party clearly realised that, in the long run, a political zero-sum-game was not in the interest of either side. Such a realisation, as we have seen earlier, was already there at the local level. As long as the provision for constituting political authority by means of the ballot box existed, it was in the interest of both sides to discard such an approach. Both party organisations now wanted to make a provision for enjoying the security of a legitimate opposition should such a need arise in the future. During the period of emergency rule and its aftermath, in certain states an attempt was made to characterise political opponents as traitors and saboteurs, invoking public wrath as a justification for possible political high-handedness. Fortunately, such tendencies did not get out of hand. Punishment for whatever was considered to be an abuse of political authority was taken out of the political arena and was handed over to judicial appointees who, despite their slowness and cumbersomeness, paid due regard to the due process of the law.

In *Political Development in the New States* (1960), Edward Shils[8] had accorded to the intellectuals in general and the political elite in particular the extraordinary role of modernising their political societies in the colonial and post-colonial period. According to Shils, they led the struggle for national independence by politically mobilising the support of the people for self-government. In the post-colonial period, they manned various state institutions to consolidate the fruits of independence.

While in the bulk of the developing countries, in the wake of national independence and afterwards, the political elite was almost totally absorbed into state machinery and in other related professions, and thereby unable to exert pressure on behalf of those who were governed, a section of the Indian political elite, right from the very start, had made a healthy beginning as critics of government and its policies or as watchdogs of the public interest. Like those in power, the critics and the watchdogs were often men of high stature, made higher in the eyes of the people by the traditional Indian value of denying oneself the prestige and power of high office. While the critics consisted of active party men, the public watchdogs were social workers, lawyers, retired judges, senior civil servants and journalists. As public criticism, which was frowned upon in the initial years of Indian democracy, increasingly acquired its legitimacy, university teachers and youth leaders also became involved in it in a big way.

Unlike most other developing countries, where the entire political elite were transformed into state functionaries, India was fortunate to have such an elite serving vital positions in government as well as in opposition. It produced critics and watchdogs, as we saw earlier, at all levels of Indian political society.

Such major strides in her democratic maturity notwithstanding, the political society of India has yet to grow out of certain self-paralysing contradictions which often result in the loss of a sense of political direction. What is basic to these contradictions is the fascination for firmness *and* civil liberties.

Three decades of evolution of Indian political society, which put a premium on civil liberties, the right to association and criticism, the independence of the judiciary, and above all on an aggressive demand for accountability verging on violence, followed by the period of emergency rule, repression in the name of discipline and the need to solve her problems in the shortest possible time and as a result make her strong, have, together, left India with a rich legacy of contradictions which are not going to be overcome in the near future. For while there is a widespread commitment to liberal values, and right down the line people have been stirred into political action in deference of such values, there is also a realisation that, given the immensity of India's problems, an administrative firmness, similar to that which was seen in the days of the emergency rule, is sorely needed. Yet the aftermath of the emergency rule has persuaded a lot of people to see its positive side as well. Such then is the state of India's political schizophrenia.

In a sense the Emergency and its aftermath of administrative laxity acted as a double catalyst. Emergency rule removed from people's minds the view that a dictatorship or an autocratic rule could be the answer to India's problems. Earlier economic problems, party defections, corruption and inefficient Congress rule had persuaded a number of people to think in terms of dictatorship as a possible solution. But the high-handedness of the period of emergency rule convinced most of them that such rule without adequate safeguards for the rights of the individual was no good either. Nevertheless, what came to be appreciated by them was the *administrative firmness* which was in evidence during the Emergency. The question before the elite and the masses was: why could not firmness in routine administration and in implementation of public policy be attempted within a democratic framework? Clearly, in formulating such a demand the people were trying to combine the best of both worlds. For them, the political alternatives represented by Indira Gandhi and Morarji Desai, of administrative firmness *or* civil liberties, one excluding the other, increasingly began to appear insufficient. In other words, the Emergency and its aftermath had catalysed political perceptions and led to demands which the party organisations and political leadership were incapable of satisfying. The political understanding of the people, enriched by the experiences of the period of emergency rule and what had followed it, had managed to stage a quantum jump, widening the gulf between their own demands and the political alternatives in which the Congress and the Janata Parties were locked. In the mature democracies of the West firmness in routine administration and in implementation of public policy does not always run counter to the enjoyment of civil liberties. Whenever it does, the courts are asked to rule on specific cases with a view to formulating general principles for future guidance. The emerging political society of India has yet to evolve the delicate balance between administrative firmness and civil liberties, one, as far as possible, not impinging on the other. Such a balance can only be worked out with the help of public men, the bureaucracy, the judiciary and the citizenry, all of them acting with a commitment to democratic values and indicating a willingness to defend them whenever the need arises.

The other major contradiction to appear in the emerging political society of India was between the giving of a mandate to govern, for a fixed period, by means of an election, and wishing to revoke it before the expiry of the term, by means of populist agitations. During the periods preceding the Emergency, and to some extent following it, a number of people involved in protest movements often took their call for the resignation of those in power as a specific political objective to be pursued by means of agitation, at times verging on violence. Within the relatively more mature democracies, however, such contradictions are confined to the demand for revoking specific legislations, which are then duly adopted by the elected chambers. During the period of excessive administrative inefficiency and corruption in India, populist political agitation, with its potential for violence, often retrieved the situation from going over the brink by forcing the elected deputies to do something to save the situation. Nevertheless, every time it was resorted to, there always remained the potential threat of not being able to return to a normal democratic process. To be able to overcome such threats, the political society needed elected representatives who were more sensitive and responsive to public demands, and a citizenry which was more actively involved in the democratic process to be able to ensure this.

7 Conclusion

The democratic process in India has followed a political sequence of its own. Given the problem of hierarchy, vast income disparity, traditional attitude to authority, and above all uncrystallised party organisations, her sequential political response has registered the following priorities: the need to build a secular and uninhibited political participation across the ethnic and religious divide; the need to make all strata of society aware of the possible instrumental use of such participation; and finally, the need to build party organisations which will work towards the realisation of its goals rather than perform managerial functions only.

The approach to political participation, its use, and the capacity to obtain the intended results from it differ from one ethnic group to another as they differ from one class to another. The social and economic background of each group together with the extent of its awareness of its own political resources determine its approach to political participation. The higher the social status and the more independent the economic base, the greater scope for uninhibited participation and exploration of the political alternatives. The lower or the less secure the social and economic status, the more restricted the scope for political participation. Furthermore, the higher the social and economic status, the greater the likelihood of a differentiated approach to political choices, the lower or the less secure the social and economic status and the greater the likelihood of group decisions.

In this study we have examined the socially uninhibited participation of the higher social economic groups such as the Brahmins, Banias and Patidars. Of the three, as we saw earlier, only the social status of the Patidars could not be determined precisely. But we also saw that the Patidar drive towards higher social recognition shifted from a claim to higher social origin to material wealth and through it to higher social status. Consequently, when these three groups participated in the democratic process, they were not unduly inhibited by the thought of their place in the social

hierarchy. Since they did not have to use their political participation to upgrade their own social positions, or build up their social
identity, right from the extension of the democratic process, they
looked for political and economic returns rather than status-
propping gains.

The case of the ethnic group below them, that of the Kshatriyas,
was different. They first of all had to establish their Kshatriya
identity. Such a pursuit in turn forced on them group considerations.
And when it came to their political participation, they found
themselves needing to trade off their political support to the
Congress Party in return for its promise to look after their economic
advancement. The Kshatriya participation in the democratic
process, in other words, was inhibited on two grounds, social and
economic. While it was relatively easier for the average Kshatriya to
overcome the limitations placed on him by the former, his freedom
from the latter required a gradual realisation on his part that in the
last analysis not the Congress Party but he himself would have to
share the burden of his economic advancement.

Initially, participation by the Christians and the Muslims was
inhibited due to historical reasons. And from independence it took
them nearly two decades to overcome it. While they feared the
possible loss of their freedom of conscience in the aftermath of the
partition of India, the Congress Party as an electioneering body –
apart from its ideological commitment to secularism – exploited
their insecurity to the fullest before each election. With the
exception of its top leadership, the main interest of the Congress
Party as an organisation was to line up the votes of the Christians
and Muslims rather than involve them in the wider democratic
process of India.

Since a large section among them had embraced Christianity or
Islam in order to circumvent the disadvantages of their former
social status, these religious minorities feared that if freedom of
conscience ended in India they might revert to their disadvan-
tageous position in the social hierarchy. Their relatively more
pronounced social identity and cohesion thus became an insurance
against a possible slide into social inferiority. For a long time after
independence they showed a marked preference for self-exclusion
rather than entering the mainstream of political life, for fear of
possible loss of status. In election after election, the bulk of them
sided with the Congress Party. But when they felt assured of the
secular future of India, their votes began to be distributed among

the different political parties. As India gained an increasing measure of democratic experience, secularism as the central issue in Indian politics began to count for less and less. For its own reasons the only political party which continued to play with it was the Congress Party. Paradoxically, by declaring itself a party deeply committed to the ideal of secularism, it used to secure the bulk of religious minority votes in most elections. The gradual assimilation of secular ideology by Indian society as a whole also meant gradual decline in support for the Congress Party on the part of the religious minorities.

It also took a few decades of political participation before the Kshatriyas, Christians and Muslims could overcome the inhibiting factor of hierarchy and/or insecurity and play a part in democratic politics. By the same token, the ex-untouchables of India, with their relatively greater sense of social humiliation and obsession with status, may take even longer. In other words, the greater the social distance, the greater the time-span of public participation needed to enter the mainstream of political life and exercise political choice in an uninhibited manner.

The democratic process, as reflected in the scholarly literature on Indian politics of the 1950s and 1960s, was expected to get bogged down in the ethnic cohesion of the various groups. But that did not happen. Instead, in its encounter with ethnic groups, the democratic process succeeded in inducing an increasingly diversified political choice within them. Nor did it get overly involved in the persisting problems of hierarchy so far as certain groups were concerned. There, too, it engendered confidence in India's secular future and created an atmosphere in which political choices were restricted less and less by the considerations of hierarchy and religious insecurity.

While such an encounter between a social organisation based on hierarchy and a democratic process based on the principle of equality was in progress, the basic economic problems of society remained in the background. This was because the non-economic problems which had their root in the traditional society claimed the attention of those involved in the democratic process. Consequently, notwithstanding the fact that the economic problems had made their presence felt in the voters' decision-making process in no uncertain terms, there was a time-lag in discovering the role of political participation as a means towards achieving specific aims.

But, again, no effective political pressure for such results could have materialised unless the considerations of hierarchy and social insecurity had run their course.

Gradually, political participation itself emerged as a secular and positive tool for achieving results, and began to interest and involve all the social groups across the ethnic divides. It also came to be perceived not merely as a periodic ritual for constituting political authority in the state and federal capitals or for obtaining verbal promises for some measures of relief, but as something of fundamental importance to the well-being of the society as a whole. Needless to say the evolution of such a perception was not a straightforward process. One of the basic questions, given the widespread corruption and floor-crossing among those who were elected, was the extent to which the voter exercised influence on his own elected deputies. The opportunity for testing it presented itself in Gujarat during the years 1974–7.

Earlier, in 1971, the Congress Party had won a landslide victory in India by promising the eradication of poverty as its principal goal. But in the years that followed the economic hardships of the common man phenomenally increased. For the average voter it was not difficult to establish a direct link between state policies and corruption in high places, and the rising cost of living. In the intense debates which often followed such a realisation the basic problem was that of what an electorate ought to do when it was convinced that its elected deputies no longer work for the welfare of those who have elected them. Should the electorate allow its deputies to complete their normal term of office or recall them by means of political agitation and *satyagraha*? The ruling Congress Party took the position that there was no provision in the constitution for recall and therefore all threats to the elected deputies must be considered undemocratic and illegitimate. The political parties opposing the Congress Party took a diametrically opposite view. They argued from a populist standpoint, as developed by Mahatma Gandhi and after him by Jayaprakash Narayan (J. P.), that in a democracy the fight to recall is implicit whether formally embodied in the constitution or not. Following such a premise, J. P. had further argued that the people even had the right to oppose government and legislature once they were convinced that these no longer worked in the common interest:

in a democracy the people, too, have the right to ask for the resignation of an elected government, if it has gone corrupt and has been misruling. And if there is a legislature that persists in supporting such a government, it too must go so that people might choose better representatives.[1]

Further:

> in a democracy the citizen has an inalienable right to civil disobedience when he finds that other channels of redress or reform have dried up. It goes without saying that the 'satayagrahi' willingly invites and accepts his lawful punishment. This is a dimension added to democracy by Gandhi. What an irony that it should be obliterated in Gandhi's own India.[2]

The question is whether such an extreme remedy for an extreme situation may not degenerate, at the hands of politically skilled dissidents, into a constantly unsettled situation. The mass upsurge in Gujarat in 1974–5, followed by the imposition of the repressive emergency period, and the election of 1977, which swept the Congress Party out of office, did not permit a dispassionate treatment of the issues involved in those four eventful years.

Theorists of democracy have argued that as a form of government it is suitable only to societies where fundamental changes of far-reaching importance are not taking place. That indeed was at the root of de Tocqueville's pessimism over the future of democracy in America.

The founding fathers of the Indian republic, too, had their own fears of the future of democracy, given the backlog of her problems. Nevertheless, they grafted a democratic political system on to a society which was in dire need of fundamental reform in the shortest possible time. All along in the national movement independence from the alien rules was identified with democracy. It was the faith and the hope of the fathers that in India democracy would not only survive but that through it the necessary social changes would also occur.

Against such a background, J. P.'s assertion that India could neither give up democracy nor allow the elected deputies, no longer working in the interest of the people, to complete their term of office, acquires special significance. J. P. saw the four eventful years as a period when *janshakti* (people's power) had to be mobilised against *rajshakti* (state power). Such a conflict was not at all desirable but it had to be resorted to in exceptional circumstances, to set things right. What was most desirable was that these two powers should work hand in hand rather than at cross-purposes. If that were possible then two of the worst features of Indian political society could be eliminated – the distance between the rulers and the ruled; and the lack of accountability of government and legislature to the people.

As far as J. P. was concerned, the protest against the misuse of state power and arbitrary rule, which began in Gujarat and Bihar in 1974–5, ought not to come to an end just because the Congress Party had been thrown out of office. What was required all the time was the need to watch the performance of those in power. He therefore proposed the formation of watchdog committees right down the line to keep in check the possible revival of irresponsible, corrupt and authoritarian rule.

The assimilation of the fall-out from those four eventful years, and its significance to political participation by the average citizen, may take years. But in the long run these will no doubt enable Indians to acquire a more searching, critical and instrumental approach to political authority as such.

The survival of the democratic process in any society depends on its ability to address itself effectively to its basic problems. But this it can do only with the help of party organisations. No matter how conscious or involved the electorate may be, it cannot take the place of party organisations. It can merely observe, evaluate and replace one party by another.

While the democratic process may be said to have struck root in India, the state of the party organisations, on which its survival depends, is far from satisfactory. The election of 1977 has revealed that so far it has not been able to break away the cycle of movement-party-movement. This can be explained as follows.

In *Parliament in India* (1957) Morris-Jones divided the evolution of the Congress Party into three phases:[3] as a pressure group, a movement, and then a political party. For all practical purposes scholars have been inclined to treat the Congress, especially after independence, *as* a political party. Occasionally attempts have been made to view it as a movement or a system.

Congress fought elections as a party but it never gave up its posture of a movement. While spearheading the struggle for independence; bringing about the integration of India after independence; introducing the ideology of democracy, secularism and socialism; putting into effect legislation for social reconstruction, industrialisation and planning; and, lastly, while introducing the emergency rule in 1975 and claiming to protect national interest, Congress in all this continued to maintain its posture as a movement.

Such a claim helped the Congress to include within itself, at all stages, groups and individuals of diverse political persuasions and commitments. Consequently, it became very difficult to unseat it with the help of any specific ideology. The Communists and Socialists, with their class-based ideology, did not get far in their plans to remove it from office.[4] Nor could the Swatantra Party, nor indeed the Jan Sangh, with their ideologies of *laissez-faire* and traditional Hinduism respectively, wrench power from it. In fact, whenever a rival political party happened to treat the Congress as a party, it could not make much headway against it.

What finally did succeed against the Congress was a rival movement, the Janata. The Congress as a movement could only be tackled by another movement. The Janata movement aimed at restoring the national heritage of democracy and civil liberty. Its goals were similar to the goals of the Congress before 1947. Like the Congress the Janata, too, contained people of diverse political persuasion. Like the Congress what it lacked was a specific programme and a group of devoted party workers to implement it.

India's social and economic problems are so immense that only political parties and party workers, deeply committed to the goal of the welfare of the common man, can provide the necessary driving force. They cannot be solved by means of periodic party-eliminating movements. After an initial success, movements tend to lose, their own sense of purpose and settle down into political parties of self-seeking individuals, thus creating the need for yet another round of movements. Such a situation can keep the cycle of movement-party-movement going for quite some time.

Only a mature electorate, together with its elite, can break such a cycle. In all stable democracies social and political movements periodically revitalise political parties by giving them fresh perspectives, new recruits and renewed political will. Such movements do not take on themselves the role of political parties. The fact that movements still assume enormous importance in developing countries goes to show that the basic political issues of civil liberties and responsive government, implicit in the struggle for national independence, are not put on a secure footing after the alien rule ends. To be able to secure them, and also sustatin the democratic process itself, it is not enough merely periodically to throw out corrupt politicians and their political parties. What is also necessary is to build and sustain political parties which make an earnest effort to get down to the basic problems of society. The electorate in India has yet to achieve this. For the democratic process in that society the creation of effective and responsive political parties has become the next item on the agenda.

Notes

1 TRADITIONAL SOCIETY THROUGH THE CRUCIBLE OF THE DEMOCRATIC PROCESS

1 Alexis de Tocqueville, *Democracy in America* (London: Longmans Green & Co., 1889) vol. I, p. 230. My italics.
2 Karl de Schweinitz, Jr, *Industrialisation and Democracy* (London: Collier-Macmillan, 1964) p. 3.
3 Ibid., pp. 10–11.
4 Ibid., p. 7.
5 S. M. Lipset, *Political Man: The Social Bases of Politics* (London: Heinemann, 1960).
6 See Philips Cutright, 'National Political Development: Social and Economic Correlates', in Nelson Polsby (ed.), *Politics and Social Life*.
7 Daniel Lerner, 'Communication Systems and Social Systems: A Statistical Exploration in History and Policy' *Behavioral Science*, 2 (1957).
8 Samuel Huntington and Joan Nelson, *No Easy Choice: Political Participation in Developing Countries* (Cambridge, Massachusetts: Harvard University Press, 1976).
9 See Talcott Parsons, 'Political Development: Times Sequences and Rates of Change' in Finkle and Gable (eds) *Political Development and Social Change*, (New York: John Wiley, 1971) p. 456.
10 Samuel J. Eldersveld, 'The Political Behaviour of the Indian Public', *Monthly Public Opinion*, vol. 9 (January 1964).
11 See in this connection I. Berlin's *The Hedgehog and the Fox* (New York: Mentor Books, 1953).
12 *Brahmins* (Dave, the rest); *Banias* (Shah, the rest); *Luhanas*; *Patidars* (Patels, Amin–Desai); *Kachhia Patel; Kshatriyas* (Gohil, Chavdas, Thakore, Parmars, the rest); *Suthars; Luhars; Sonis; Vallands; Dobhi; Barot; Mochi; Kumbhars; Darji; Backward castes* (LC); Scheduled castes; Scheduled Tribes; *Christians* (Christians, Christy); *Muslims* (Vohra, the rest); *Sindhis; Marwadis; Non-Gujaratis* (North, South and West); Miscellaneous.
13 In 1971, 1972 and 1975, 27, 28 and 35 persons respectively had to be substituted as some of the people in the sample had either moved away, become untraceable or had died. Wherever possible a son, daughter, brother, sister or neighbour was substituted for the missing or the dead respondent, always from the same caste, sex and neighbourhood.
14 Daniel Lerner, 'Communication Systems and Social Systems: Statistical Exploration in History and Policy', *Behavioral science*, 2 (1957).
15 See in this connection Lee Siegelman, *Modernization and the Political System: A*

Critique and Preliminary Empirical Analysis (Beverley Hills, California: Sage Publication, 1971).

16 See the *Gazetteer of the Bombay Presidency* (Bombay: Government Central Press, 1879) vol. III, pp. 29–37. Also David Pocock, *Kanbi and Patidar* (Oxford: Oxford University Press, 1972).

17 See in this connection, A. M. Shah and R. G. Shroff 'The Vahivancha Barots of Gujarat: A Case of Genealogists and Mythographers', in *Traditional India: Structure and Change* (Philadelphia: Milton Singer (ed.), American Folklore Society, 1959) p. 62.

18 M. N. Srinivas, *Social Change in Modern India* (Berkeley: California University Press, 1966) pp. 96–101.

19 Purshottam Shah and Chandrakant Shah (eds), *Charotar Seva Sangraha* (Nadiad: Lokmat Prakashan Ltd, 1954) p. 792.

20 A. M. Shah, 'Political System in Eighteenth Century Gujarat', in *Enquiry*, vol. I, (Spring 1964) p. 94.

21 Shah and Shah (eds), op. cit., p. 792.

22 This view was expressed to me personally by Bhailalbhai Patel, the Great Patidar leader, who belonged to Sojitra and had a lively interest in Patidar social history.

23 D. F. Pocock, 'The Hypergamy of the Patidars', *Professor Ghurye Felicitation Volume* (Bombay: Popular Book Depot, 1954) p. 198.

24 See in this connection S. Rudolph and L. Rudolph, *Modernity of Tradition* (Chicago: Chicago University Press, 1967) pp. 34–6.

25 For the regional composition of the Muslims at the turn of the century see *The Gazetteer of the Bombay Presidency* pp. 36–7.

26 See in this connection, A. H. Somjee and G. Somjee 'Co-operative Dairying and the Profiles of Social Change in India' *Economic Development and Cultural Change*, vol. 26, no. 3 (April, 1978).

2 SOCIAL COHESION AND THE DECLINE OF POLITICAL HOMOGENEITY

1 I am grateful to the editors of the *American Political Science Review* for their kind permission to include portions of my paper 'Caste and the Decline of political Homogeneity', originally published in vol. LXVII, no. 3 (September, 1973).

2 See Max Weber, 'Class, Status, Party' in H. H. Gerth and C. Wright Mills (eds), *From Max Weber: Essays in Sociology*, (London: Kegan Paul, Trench, Trubner & Co., 1947) p. 189.

3 See in this connection Donald L. Horowitz, 'Three Dimensions of Ethnic Politics', *World Politics*, vol. 23, no. 2 (January 1971) p. 233.

4 Gerth and Mills, op. cit., p. 189.

5 For the details of the interaction between traditional society based on the principle of hierarchy and the new political system based on the principle of equality, within the framework of an empirically testable situation, see my *Democracy and Political Change in Village India* (New Delhi: Orient Longman, 1972).

6 Robert Dahl, *Who Governs?* (New Haven: Yale University Press, 1961) p. 59.

7 Raymond E. Wolfinger, 'The Development and Persistence of Ethnic Voting',

American Political Science Review, vol. LIX (1965) p. 905.

8 Michael Parenti, 'Ethnic Politics and the Persistence of Ethnic Identification,' *American Political Science Review*, vol. LXI (1967) p. 718.

9 Nathan Glazer and Daniel P. Moynihan, *Beyond the Melting Pot* (Cambridge, Massachusetts: MIT Press, 1963) p. 1.

10 M. N. Srinivas, *Caste in Modern India and Other Essays* (Bombay: Asia Publishing House, 1962) pp. 15, 16.

11 Ibid., p. 16.

12 Ibid., p. 2.

13 Selig Harrison, *India: The Most Dangerous Decades* (Princeton: Princeton University Press, 1960) pp. 211–12.

14 The figures provided by Harrison did not conclusively establish his thesis of caste-party identity. On the contrary they presented us with a picture of party inroads into castes. There were obviously more Kammas to go round for both the parties, and subsequently Kammas as well as Reddis concentrated on the Congress. See Harrison, op. cit., pp. 211, 212 and 219.

15 See Myron Weiner, *The Politics of Scarcity: Public Pressure and Political Response in India* (Chicago: University of Chicago Press, 1962) p. 37.

16 Ibid., pp. 37–8; my italics.

17 No one knows exactly what the total number of castes in India is. There are certain genuine difficulties: the problem of determining the status of breakaway fragments of castes, the social mobility of certain sections of them, migrations and the emergence of sectional identity, uncontrolled assimilation of the groups of Adivasis into the Hindu social organisations, etc. It is virtually impossible to keep track of these continuing processes across the entire Indian sub-continent, together with the areas of Indian migrations, and arrive at a definite figure for the total number of castes. The rough total given above is taken from Robert Hardgrave's *The Nadars of Tamilnad* (Berkeley: University of California Press, 1969). He maintained: 'There are in India more than three thousand castes, each culturally distinct endogamous community sharing traditionally a common occupation and a particular position in the localized hierarchy of caste ranking' (p. 2).

18 Lloyd I. Rudolph and Susanne Hoeber Rudolph, *The Modernity of Tradition* (Chicago: University of Chicago Press, 1967) p. 62.

19 Ibid., p. 103.

20 Ibid., p. 62.

21 Ibid., pp. 27–8.

22 Disputing Marx's thesis that the British rule in India would eventually lead to the atomisation of even Indian villages and castes, the Rudolphs argue that 'India has shown a strong propensity to transform rather than supersede traditional corporate structures, to move imperceptibly from traditional to modern corporatism without so marked an intervening individualist phase as the West is said to have experienced' (Rudolph and Rudolph, op. cit., p. 23; my italics).

23 Ibid., pp. 24–6.

24 Ibid., pp. 25–6.

25 Ibid., p. 97.

26 Ibid., pp. 34–6.

27 Ibid., pp. 29–36.

28 Rajni Kothari and Rushikesh Maru, 'Federating for Political Interests: The Kshatriyas of Gujarat' in Rajni Kothari (ed.), *Caste in Indian Politics* (New Delhi: Orient Longman Ltd, 1970) pp. 70–101.

29 Harold Gould, 'Adaptive Functions of Caste in Contemporary Indian Society,' *Asian Survey*, 3 (September 1963) pp. 427–38.

30 M. N. Srinivas has used the term 'Sankritisation' in order to indicate a number of means used in order to gain recognition for higher social status. One of these is a conscious attempt to conform to and be seen as conforming to higher ritual standards. See in this connection his *Social Change in Modern India* (Berkeley: University of California Press, 1966) p. 6.

31 See the fascinating paper by William Rowe, 'The New Cauhans: A Caste Mobility Movement in North India' in James Silverberg (ed.), *Social Mobility in the Caste System in India*, (The Hague: Mouton, 1968); also Srinivas, *Social Change in Modern India*, pp. 1–45.

32 See F. G. Bailey, *Caste, Tribe and Nation* (Manchester: Manchester University Press, 1960).

33 Paul Lazarsfeld, Bernard Berelson and Hazel Gaudet, *The People's Choice* (New York: Columbia University Press, 1968) p. 151.

34 M. N. Srinivas first used the expression 'vote-bank' in connection with the political influence of patron over client. See his paper 'The Social System of a Mysore Village' in McKim Marriot (ed.), *Village India: Studies in the Little Community*, (Chicago: University of Chicago Press, 1955). Later F. G. Bailey used the expression in order to refer to the electoral influence of the caste leader. See his *Politics and Social Change* (Berkeley: University of California Press, 1959).

35 For a detailed account of this process, see A. H. Somjee 'Political Dynamics of a Gujarat Village,' *Asian Survey*, vol. 12 (July 1972) pp. 602–8.

36 For a detailed empirical support for the theory of stimulus-response within the framework of political emulation see A. H. Somjee, *Democracy and Political Change in Village India: A Case Study* (New Delhi: Orient Longman, 1972).

37 See Chapter VII, 'Village Politics and National Politics: The General Election of 1967' in A. H. Somjee, *Democracy and Political Change in Village India*.

38 This indicates the participation of the families of respondents in previous elections.

39 For the details of this see Rajni Kothari and Rushikesh Maru, 'Caste and Secularism in India: Case Study of a Caste Federation,' *Journal of Asian Studies*, 25 (November 1965), pp. 33–50.

3   THE THREE ELECTORAL GENERATIONS

1 David Butler and Donald Stokes, *Political Change in Britain* (London: Macmillan, 1969) p. 65.

2 Ibid., p. 66.

3 Ibid., p. 67.

4 Ibid., p. 68.

5 See Bernard R. Berelson, Paul F. Lazarsfeld and William N. McPhee, *Voting* (Chicago: University of Chicago Press, fifth impression 1966) p. 302. My italics.

6 Ibid., p. 301.

7 See *Public Opinion Quarterly*, vol. 23 (Spring 1959) pp. 63–72.
8 Ibid., p. 66.
9 Ibid., p. 68.
10 Ibid., p. 68.
11 See 'The Problem of Generations' in Karl Mannheim, *Essays on the Sociology of Knowledge* (London: Routledge & Kegan Paul, 1952) p. 282.
12 Ibid., pp. 282–3.
13 Ibid., p. 290.
14 Maurice Zetlin tried to periodise generations *within* the Cuban working class. See in this connection his 'Political Generations in the Cuban Working Class', in *American Journal of Sociology*, vol. 71 (1965–6) pp. 493–508.
15 Ibid., p. 303.
16 Ibid., p. 303.
17 For the concept of generation and its specific uses see the following: David Butler and Donald Stokes, *Political Change in Britain*; F. G. Greenstein, *Children and Politics* (New Haven: Yale University Press, 1965); M. Benny, A. P. Gray and R. H. Pear, *How People Vote* (London: Routledge & Kegan Paul, 1956); Robert McKenzie and Allan Silver, *Angels in Marble* (London: Heinemann, 1968); S. N. Eisenstadt, *From Generation to Generation* (London: Routledge & Kegan Paul, 1956); S. M. Lipset, *Political Man* (London: Heinemann, 1960); Bennet M. Berger, 'How long is a Generation?' *British Journal of Sociology*, vol. 11 (1960); Maurice Zetlin, op. cit.; M. Kent Jennings and Richard G. Niemi, 'The Transmission of Political Values from Parent to Child' *American Political Science Review*, vol. 62 (March 1968); Marvin Rintala, 'A Generation in Politics: A Definition' *Review of Politics*, vol. 25 (October 1963); Neal R. Cutler, 'Generation, Maturation, and Party Affiliation: A Cohort Analysis' *Public Opinion Quarterly*, vol. 33 (1969); Julian Marias and Marvin Rintala, 'Generations', *Encyclopedia of the Social Sciences*, vol. 6; and Joseph R. Gusfields, 'The Problem of Generations in an Organizational Structure', *Social Forces*, vol. 35 (1956–7).
18 In 1975, we had added fifty additional first-time voters to our sample. At appropriate points in this chapter we shall include analyses of their perspectives, evaluations and votes.
19 See for the exposition of this concept William M. Evan, 'Cohort Analysis of Survey Data'.
20 Butler and Stokes, *op. cit.*, p. 58.
21 See in this connection S. M. Lipset's 'Students and Politics in Comparative Perspective', *Daedalus* (Winter 1968) p. 3.
22 See Paul F. Lazarsfeld, Bernard Berelson and Hazel Gaudet, *The People's Choice* (New York: Columbia University Press, 1948) p. 25.
23 See Edward Shils, 'Indian Students: Rather Sadhus than Philistines' in Philip Altbach (ed.), *Turmoil and Transition*, (New York: Basic Books, 1968) p. 91.
24 On the eve of the Assembly election of 1975, we had added yet another fifty first-time voters, who were then clubbed together in the category of 'young generation'. With the passage of time all the segments in the middle generation had advanced in age. Consequently, after 1975, we treated the middle and old generations as one group.

4 ECONOMIC SELF-PERCEPTION AND POLITICAL RESPONSE

1 Barrington Moore, Jr, *Social Origins of Dictatorship and Democracy* (London: Allen Lane, 1966), pp. 369–70.
2 The term 'new political system' refers to the democratic political system.
3 Ralf Dahrendorf, *Class and Class Conflict in Industrial Society* (London: Routledge & Kegan Paul, 1959) p. 8.
4 See in this connection an unfinished note on class by Karl Marx in *Capital: A Critique of Political Economy*, vol. III (Moscow: Foreign Languages Publishing House, 1959) p. 863.
5 Dahrendorf, *op. cit.*, p. 19.
6 See in this connection 'Karl Marx's Theory of Social Classes' in R. Bendix and S. M. Lipset (eds), *Class, Status and Power*, (New York: The Free Press, second edition 1966) p. 8.
7 Even in nineteenth-century Europe and America, with their growing industrialisation and urbanisation and the lessening isolation of the economically poor, the struggle for their economic advancement was a very slow process indeed. See in this connection an excellent paper, by Asa Briggs, 'The Language of Class in Early Nineteenth Century England' in Asa Briggs and John Saville (eds), *Essays in Labour History*, (London: Macmillan, 1967).
8 Karl Marx, *The Eighteenth Brumaire of Louis Bonaparte* (New York: International Publishers, 1963) p. 123.
9 See Max Weber 'Class, Status, Party' in H. H. Garth and C. Wright Mills (eds), *From Max Weber: Essays in Sociology* (London: Kegan Paul, Trench, Trubner & Co., Ltd., 1947) p. 185.
10 Dahrendorf, *op. cit.*, p. 14.
11 Ibid., p. 17.
12 Ibid., p. 57.
13 T. B. Bottomore *Classes in Modern Society* (London: Allen & Unwin, 1965) p. 27.
14 See in this connection Max Weber's incisive paper, 'Class, Status, Party' in Gerth and Wright Mills (eds), op. cit., pp. 188–9.
15 See for a detailed account of this process my *Democracy and Political Change in Village India* (New Delhi: Orient Longman, 1972).
16 In contrast to the Congress Party, the Swatantra Party stood for a greater measure of private and unrestricted economic activity.
17 Jan Sangh's economic policies were not always clearly stated. In broad terms it favoured private enterprise with as few restrictions as possible.

5 PARTY ORGANISATION, CAMPAIGNING AND VOTER CONTACT

1 Robert R. Alford, *Party and Society: The Anglo-American Democracies* (New York: Rand McNally & Co., 1964) pp. X–XI.
2 See S. M. Lipset, *The Political Man: The Social Bases of Politics* (London: Heinemann, 1960) pp. 63–4.
3 J. Goldthorpe, D. Lockwood, F. Bechhoffer and J. Platt, *The Affluent Worker:*

Industrial Attitudes and Behaviour (Cambridge: Cambridge University Press, 1968) pp. 174–86.

4 See in this connection Robert MacKenzie and Allan Silver, *Angel in Marble: Working Class Conservatives in Urban England* (London: Heinemann, 1968) p. vi.

5 S. M. Lipset and S. Rokkan (eds), *Party System and Voter Alignments* (New York: The Free Press, 1967); see the Introduction.

6 W. H. Morris-Jones, 'Dominance and Dissent: Their Inter-relations in the Indian Party System' *Government and Opposition*, vol. I (1965–6) p. 455.

7 Ibid., p. 455.

8 Op. cit., p. 455.

9 Avery Leiserson, *Parties and Politics* (New York: Knopf, 1958) p. 177.

10 Myron Weiner, *Party Building in a New State* (Chicago: Chicago University Press, 1967) p. 15.

11 S. J. Eldersveld, *Political Parties: A Behavioral Analysis* (Chicago: Rand McNally & Co., 1964) p. 1.

12 See in this connection G. A. Almond and G. B. Powell, *Comparative Politics: A Development Approach* (Boston: Little, Brown & Co., 1966) pp. 98–128.

13 Kay Lawson, *The Comparative Study of Political Parties* (New York: St Martin's Press, 1976).

14 See in this connection Morton Grodzin's paper, 'Political Parties and the Crisis of Succession in the United States: The Case of 1800,' in Joseph LaPalombara and Myron Weiner (eds), *Political Parties and Political Development* (Princeton: Princeton University Press, 1966) pp. 317–23.

15 For want of a better expression, I have used the term 'operational linkage' in order to indicate the diversity of motivations and pursuits among men *actually* involved in linkage activity.

16 In the Indian situation, the marginals are often drawn from the ranks of lawyers, businessmen, industrialists, ethnic and religious leaders and men of means and influence generally.

17 See in this connection Arend Lijphart, *The Politics of Accommodation: Pluralism and Democracy in the Netherlands* (Berkeley: California University Press, 1968), particularly his model for explaining the politics of accommodation within a society with 'an extraordinary degree of social cleavage' (p. 2), building minimal political consensus round 'programmatic solutions' (p. 103).

18 From my field-work notes, January 1967. Campaign meeting attended by me in the village of Gamadi, near Anand.

19 From my field-work notes, January 1967. Campaign meeting attended in the village of Sojitra, near Anand.

20 From my field-work notes, March 1971. Campaign meeting attended in Anand.

21 Morarji Desai, *Facts You Must Know* (1971).

22 See in this connection my paper 'Rationality, Conformity, and Frivolity in Indian Elections', *Political Studies* (December 1971).

6   AN EMERGING POLITICAL SOCIETY

1 Gabriel A. Almond and Sidney Verba, *The Civic Culture: Political Attitudes and Democracy in Five Nations* (Boston: Little, Brown & Co., 1963).

2 Lucian W. Pye and Sidney Verba (eds), *Political Culture and Political Development* (Princeton, N.J.: Princeton University Press, 1965).
3 See in this connection the definition of culture by Alfred L. Kroeber and Clyde Kluckohn on p. 95 of George A. Theodorson and Achilles G. Theodorson, *A Modern Dictionary of Sociology* (London: Metheun, 1970):

> culture consists of patterns, explicit and implicit, of and for behavior acquired and transmitted by symbols, constituting the distinctive achievements of human groups, in including their embodiments in artifacts; the essential core of culture consists of traditional (i.e., historically derived and selected) ideas and especially their attached values.

4 'India: Two Political Cultures' in Pye and Verba, op. cit., pp. 199–200.
5 S. P. Huntington and J. M. Nelson, *No Easy Choice: Political Participation in Developing Countries* (Cambridge, Mass.: Harvard University Press, 1976) pp. 28–9.
6 See Robert Dahl, *Polyarchy: Participation and Opposition* (New Haven: Yale University Press, 1971) pp. 2–8.
7 There is an interesting form of politico-economic mobilisation also going on in rural Gujarat in the form of the highly successful milk co-operative moment. An exposure to such a movement has brought about social change in various areas of rural life. See in this connection, A. H. Somjee and G. Somjee, 'Cooperative Dairying and the Profiles of Social Change in India', *Economic Development and Cultural Change* (April 1978).
8 Edward Shils, *Political Development in the New States* (The Hague: Mouton & Company, 1960).

7 CONCLUSION

1 Jayaprakash Narayan, 'Testament of Protest' *Far Eastern Economic Review*, (20 February 1976) p. 21.
2 Ibid., p. 22.
3 W. H. Morris-Jones, *Parliament in India* (London: Longmans Green, 1957) pp. 167–75.
4 For the role of the Congress as a movement and its success in preventing the growth of an effective socialist party see Geeta Somjee, 'An Examination of the Socialist Concerns, Critiques, Agitations and Organisational Attempts within the Indian National Movement', (Ph.D. thesis, 'University of Baroda, 1978).

Index

AMUL (Kaira District Co-operative Milk Producers' Union), 17, 29–30, 88, 105
Accommodation, inter-party, 11, 110–13
Accountability of leaders, 12, 80, 99, 137, 149–51; increasing pressure for, 90, 100, 134–5, 140, 151
Adaptive structures, 34, 40, 105
Age groups, *see* Generations
Agitation, political, 83–4, 92, 100, 132, 140, 144–5, 149–51
Agriculturalists, rise to power, 7; status, 89; unionisation, 135; voting, 96–7
Agriculture, in Anand, 29–30
Agriculture, Institute of, 28
Alford, Robert, 101–2
Almond, G. A., 126
Amery Hospital, Anand, 24
Amin clan, 20
Amin, Motibhai, 27
Anand, 12, 13, 17, 88; agriculture, 29–30; Banias, 18–19; Brahmins, 17–18, 19; Christians, 24–5; cleavage structures, 18; economic development, 22, 29–30, 79; education, 27–9; electoral generations, 68; ethnic groups, 17–26; institutions, 26–30; Kshatriyas, 22–4; municipality, 18, 26–7; Muslims, 25–6; Patidars, 17, 18, 19–22; study: interviews, 15, purpose, 14, 15–16, sample, 13, 15, time-scale, 13–14; trades unions, 88
Anand Printing Press, 25
Andhra state, 35–6
Assembly elections, *see* Elections
Attitudes, political, 135–8

Bajkhedawal, 17

Bangladesh crisis, 57, 136
Banias, in Anand, 18–19; canvassing, 123; and democracy, 131 137, 138; and firm leadership, 138; status, 89, 131, 146–7; voting, 19, 49–61, 137
Banking, nationalisation, 56
Bendix, R., 85
Berelson, Bernard R., 64, 102
Bhadaran village, 21
Birth control, 26, 77, 78
Blame, apportionment of, 79–80
Bombay Municipal Act, 1884, 18
Brahmins, in Anand, 17–18, 19; canvassing, 123; and firm leadership, 138; political participation, 131, 137, 138; status, 18, 89, 131, 146–7; voting, 18, 49–61, 137
Businessmen, voting, 96
Butler, David, 63, 75

CES, *see* Charotar Education Society
Campaign tactics, 114–24; businessmen, mobilisation of, 115; canvassing, 121–4; cash, 118–19; intimidation, 115; literature, 119–21; paid workers, 115; rumour, 118–19; speeches, 115–18
Candidates, 114, 115–18
Canvassing, 121–4
Caste, aims, primary, 34, 40–1, 42, 43, 44; associations and social cohesion, 34, 37–8, 40, 47, 49; and candidates, 114; and class, 83, 89; communication networks, 37, 40; councils, 34, 42, 44; decision-making, 44–6; and democracy, 33–5, 46, 130–2, 146–8; and endogamy, 34, 35, 40, 41, 42, 43; and ethnicity, 31, 87; federations, 40; hierarchy, 87; honour, 31, 87, 89,

India, agriculturalists, importance of, 7–8; attitudes, political, 135–8; British *raj*, 18, 85, 87; caste, and democracy, 33–46, 89, 130–2; citizenship, common, 8, 87; class conflict, 82–4, 85–6, 92; economic development, 2, 5, 13–14, 54; economic rights, 87, 89, 91, 135; elections, *see* Elections: generations, electoral, 68–75; hardship, 79, 97–8; hierarchical social structure, 7, 8, 83, 87–90; institutions, democratic, 13, 68, 82, 87, 125–6, 133, 136–7, 139–42; inter-party relations, 103, 110–13, 152; local government, 46–8; mobilisation, political, 11–12, 129, 132–5; nationalism, 10, 22, 82, 132, 133, 141; partition, 25; political participation, belief in, 5–6; political society, 11–12, 16, 125–6, 126–7, 129–45; populism, 100, 144–5, 149; rural democracy, 46–8, 133, 135; secularism, 52–3, 58, 62, 91, 129–32, 147–8; social change, movement for, 9–10, 83; socio-political system, 33, 34

Institutions, democratic, 2–4, 13, 68, 82, 87, 125–6, 128–9, 133, 134, 136–7, 139–42

Interest linkage, 10, 107–8

Intimidation, and voting, 115

Irish Presbyterian Mission, 24–5

Issues, social, differing importance, 76–8; identification of, 77; perception of, 76–81

J. P., *see* Narayan, Jayaprakash

Janata Party, 58, 117, 130, 144; and Banias, 59, 61; and Brahmins, 59, 61; campaign literature, 120, 121; and Christians, 59, 61; and Congress Party, 117–18, 152; and democracy, 142; and housewives, 95; and Kshatriyas, 59, 61; and Muslims, 59, 61; and Patidars, 59, 61

Jan Sangh Party, Assembly election, *1972*, 57–8, 70; candidates, 57, 114; and Congress Party, 120, 152; leadership, 138; right-wing nature, 55, 59,

120; and youth, 73, 75, 76

Jats, 37, 39

Jones, W. H. Morris-, *see* Morris-Jones, W. H.

Judiciary, and democracy, 142, 144

Juvanias, 27

KMLP, *see* Kisan Majdoor Lok Paksh Party

Kaira district, 19, 50

Kaira District Co-operative Milk Producers' Union, *see* AMUL

Kanabi clan, 20

Karamsad village, 21

Key, V. O., 117

Kin-group neighbourhood, 44–5

Kisan Majdoor Lok Paksh Party (KMLP), 58; and Banias, 59; and Brahmins, 59; canvassing, 123; and Christians, 59; and Kshatriyas, 59; and Muslims, 59; and Patidars, 59

Kothari, R., 103

Kshatriyas, in Anand, 22–4; as candidates, 26, 52, 57, 114; canvassing, 123; caste associations, 37, 39 (*see also* Sabha; Samaj); employment, 23; and firm government, 138; hierarchy, 23; leaders, 131–2; political differentiation, 49; political participation, 49, 52, 131–2, 137, 138; rural politics, 46–8; social mobility, 23; status, 89, 131, 147; urban politics, 49–61; voting, 23–4, 46, 49–61, 93

Kshatriya Sabha, *see* Sabha

Kshatriya Seva Samaj, *see* Samaj

Kurien, V., 29

Land Tenancy Act, 23, 50, 51, 97

Leadership, attitudes to, 138, 141; bifurcated, 43–4, 45, 47, 48; caste, 42, 43–4; charismatic figures, 56, 72, 141; firm, 138, 143–4; political, 44, 47, 48, 111, 131; social, 44, 47

Legislation, implementation, 9, 91

Leiserson, Avery, 104, 105

Lerner, Daniel, 4, 16

Liberty, civil, and firm government, 12, 143–4

Life-cycle, political, 63–4

Linkage, interest, 10, 107–8; and inter-party accommodation, 110–13; normative, 107, 108–9; operational, 107, 109–10; and party organisation, 10–11, 107–10; types, 107–10
Lipset, S. M., 4, 6, 75, 85, 102
Literacy, 16, 49
Literature, election campaign, 119–21
Local government, 46–8
Lockwood, D., 102
Lok Paksh Party, 49; and Patidars, 49–50
Lokshahi, 136–7

Mackenzie, Robert, 75, 102
Mahagujarat Janata Parishad, 50
Mahida, Narendrasingh, 116
Maintenance of Internal Security Act, 80–1
Maleks, 25
Manipulation model of party organisation, 104–5
Mannheim, Karl, 65–7
Marriage and social advancement, 21
Marx, Karl, 9; class, concept of, 83, 84–7, 92
Media, in decision-making, 45
Medicine, in Anand, 24
Mehta, Balwantrai, 133
Milk co-operatives, *see* AMUL
Mobilisation, political, 11–12, 49, 52, 129, 132–5
Moghuls, 25
Molesalams, 25
Momnas, 25
Montesquieu, Baron de, 2–3
Moore, Barrington, Jr., 4, 9, 82
Morris-Jones, W. H., 103, 110–11, 151
mota gams, 20–1, 111–12
mota mota loko, 92
Movements, political, and parties, 151–2
Moynihan, Daniel, 33
Mukti Foj, *see* Salvation Army
Munshi, K. M., 29
Muslims, in Anand, 25–6; and family planning, 78; and firm leadership, 138; political participation, 131, 137,

138; voting, 25–6, 49, 52, 53, 54–5, 93, 137, 147–8

Nadars, 37, 39
Nadiad village, 21
Narayan, Jayaprakash (J. P.), 60, 117, 133, 149, 150–1
Nationalism, 10, 22, 82, 132, 133, 141
Navnirman Movement, 58, 60, 80, 117, 130, 137
Navroji, Dadabhai, 28
Nehru, Jawaharlal, 5, 25, 72, 90, 133, 141
Nelson, Joan, 4–5, 132
Normative linkage, 107, 108–9

Occupations, and voting, 94–8, 131
Old, the, *see* Generations
Operational linkage, 107, 109–10
Organisation Congress Party, and Banias, 55–6, 57; and Brahmins, 55–6, 57; and businessmen, 96; campaign literature, 120; and Christians, 55–6, 57; elections: *1971*, 55–6, 70, *1972*, 73; and Kshatriyas, 55–6, 57; leadership, 138; and Muslims, 55–6, 57; and Patidars, 55–6, 57; and youth, 75
Organisation, social, interaction with political system, 88–90

Panchayats, 34, 44
Parenti, Michael, 32–3
Parmar clan, 23
Parsons, Talcott, 6, 33, 34, 106
Party organisations, activists, 10, 109–10, 112, 113, 153; broad-based support, 6, 7, 11; campaigning, 114–20; functions: 88, 104–5, 107–10, 151–2, between elections, 10–11, 103–4, 107, 108, 110, 113; inter-party relations, 103, 110–13, 152; linkage, 10–11, 107–10; linkmen, 109–10; marginals, 10, 109–10, 112, 113; models, 101–13; paid workers, 115; voter contact, 121–4
Patel clan, 20
Patel, Bhailalbhai, 29, 50
Patel, Sardar, 29, 141

Swatantra Party, 51, 70, Anand
Municipality elections, 26–7; and
Banias, 51, 53; and Brahmins, 51, 53;
and businessmen, 96; campaign
literature, 119; and Christians, 54;
and Congress Party, 104, 111, 112,
152; economic policy, 94, 116; and
education in Anand, 29; and
Kshatriyas, 24, 51, 52, 53, 94; and
Muslims, 54–5; and Patidars, 51–2,
53, 94
Syeds, 25

T. K., *see* Patel, Tribhuvandas
Tais, 25
Thakur clan, 23
Tocqueville, Alexis de, 3, 125, 150
Trades unions, 88, 135
Traits, political, 127

Unemployment, 77, 78, 97
Unionisation, *see* Trades unions
United States, democracy in, 3; ethnic
voting, 32–3; Watergate problem,
108–9, 129
Urbanisation and democracy, 4, 16,
48–61

Vasavas, 46, 47
Vaso village, 21
Venkars, 46, 47
Verba, Sidney, 126
Vidyanagar, 12, 51, 52
Vithal Udyognagar, 30
Vohras, 25, 131
Voting, and age, *see* Generations; and
canvassing, 121–4; and class, 102;
economic rationale for, 93–4; and
economic self-perception, 92–100;
ethnic, 32–3, 45; and income, 98;
increasing discrimination, 116, 133–
4; influences on, 73–4, 114–20; and
occupation, 94–8; secret ballot, 118;
urban, 49–61

Weber, Max, 31, 86, 89
Weiner, Myron, 36–7, 104–5, 110, 126
Wolfinger, Raymond, 32
Women, voting, 95–6

Youth, and Congress Party, 69, 73, 74,
75, 76; and Jan Sangh Party, 73, 75,
76; political agitation, 100; voting,
59–60, 73